Let's Talk About It !

Written and illustrated by
Joe Wayman

Cover by Tom Sjoerdsma

Copyright ©Good Apple, Inc., 1986

ISBN No. 0-86653-372-9

Printing No. 987654321

GOOD APPLE, INC.
299 JEFFERSON ROAD
P.O. BOX 480
PARSIPPANY, NJ 07054-0480

✳contents

SPRINGBOARDS INTO LANGUAGE
SOME HELPFUL HINTS

The activity units in this book are designed to be "springboards" or "jumping-off" places into units of study. They are motivational in nature and not intended to stand on their own. They should be used to motivate the **use** and **development** of **language skills** through a variety of content areas. Use these units with your current curriculum and in conjunction with the material you are already teaching. They will stimulate your learners and bring them to higher levels of involvement.

The development of language comes with the **uses of language in an interactive setting and in a purposeful manner**. What we are seeing in our young today is a frightening deterioration in the use of oral language. The research tells us that students spend close to eighty percent of their time in schools **listening**; and if that were not bad enough, they then go home and experience a family setting dominated by television . . . and again spend large chunks of time being "speechless." Our children need to **talk, talk, talk**. And they need to do it in relation to a variety of thinking skills and in a variety of learning environments.

The activities in this book will encourage the use of oral language predominantly as students, in partners, trios and small group settings, are invited to:

EXPLAIN	DISCUSS	COMPROMISE
DEFINE	CONFRONT	CREATE
DESCRIBE	DECIDE	CONCLUDE
QUESTION	CLARIFY	

The use of one or two of these activities each day will help develop fluent, confident speakers—students who can defend ideas, think on their feet and express themselves verbally. Use these activities in conjunction with your curriculum, or let students do them on their own.

At the beginning of each unit you will find a listing of content areas with which that unit can be easily coordinated.

There is no "order" to the units in this book. The unit on ducks might fit into a study of birds, the unit on flowers into a botany unit and the unit on heads into social studies. Many of the activities will lead not only into oral expression but also into story writing, vocabulary development, and poetry. In almost all cases students will be working **with someone else**. . . not in isolation.

Evaluation? No. You can't evaluate these experiences. While you may evaluate or grade the **products** of these experiences, please **do not** try to evaluate the experience itself. Instead, ask students to begin to **self-evaluate** these experiences. Did you like it? How did it make you feel? Why was it uncomfortable for you? Do you think this kind of thing is important? Why? Why not? Would you do it again? How would you like to do it differently? Why do you think we are doing these kinds of activities? Would you like to do more or less of this kind of thing?

RATIONALE

In the research on learning, we find over and over again that learning is dependent upon some very elusive elements:

Intrinsic motivation: We learn best when "we" want to learn . . . for **ourselves**, not for someone else.

Desire: No one can create desire in another human being. But we can do everything possible to stimulate that desire, then cross our fingers and hope it happens.

Involvement: The higher the levels of involvement the more likely we are to trigger motivation and desire. The levels of involvement may be viewed as being the following for the purposes of this book:

Visual: Using pictures or images

Imagination: Using guided imagination to trigger motivation

Communication: Oral expression . . . talking to each other and interacting in a small . . . low risk . . . group

Touch, taste, sound, smell, and physical movement: Each of these increases the level of involvement for the learner.

In this book you will find no duplicatable pages, no ditto masters, no fill in the blanks. Learning is dying because of an overabundance of this kind of mindless and deadening nonlearning kind of experience. Each of these units requires active involvement and participation with all of the senses. They will ask both **you** and your **students** to come alive, experience the excitement and thrill of discovering language through the active use of it! Hence the title **Let's Talk About It!** If language truly comes alive for your students they will choose to use it and grow with it for the rest of their lives. Can we ask for more?

Sincerely,

Joe Wayman

OBJECTIVES

1. Students will spend time each day **talking** with each other with a specific purpose or goal.
2. Students will **explain** or **describe** something in detail or to the satisfaction of a partner.
3. Students will **compromise** in an attempt to reach a group decision.
4. Students will convert or communicate into images and will convert images into oral communication.
5. Students will **clarify** through the use of oral expression ideas to one or more partners.
6. Students will **decide** and communicate their decisions to a partner or partners.
7. Students will eventually be comfortable addressing the entire group and be able to verbalize ideas to the class while "thinking on their feet."
8. Students will be able to **see** and **verbally explain** relationships between things, concepts, or ideas.
9. Students will both **give** and **follow** directions.
10. Students will **plan**, **organize** and follow through on projects reaching conclusions and bringing closure to specific tasks.
11. Students will be asked to be **fluent**, **flexible**, and **associative in their thinking, thus encouraging more creative thought.**

HOW MANY WAYS?

Coordinate with:

Language arts
Sentence structure
Any content area
Storytelling

①

This activity teaches sentence structure as well as fluency and flexibility with the language. Students love it and the results can be spectacular.

First you will need to generate a fairly simple sentence to write on the board. Use a student's sentence or one the class creates on the spot. The sentence should be similar in structure to the example on the following pages.

Write it on the board and draw vertical lines between each part of speech all the way to the bottom of the board. Make prepositional phrases one section and adjectives such as **the** part of the word they describe. Explain to your class that you are going to brainstorm all the other things or words that could be used in each vertical column instead of the one that is there. The sky is the limit! Use your imagination! There is one rule:

• The word or phrase for each column must be of parallel construction with the word or phrase at the top. In other words, the number, tense and form must be the same. You may wish to discuss these three elements before proceeding.

First, what are all the words you could use besides the word **black** in this sentence? List them. Some examples might be: tired, sleek, gray, silent, etc.

Second, under cat, what are all the other things this sentence could be about? List them: dog, dragon, shoe, troll, mouse, etc.

Do this for each section of the sentence. Now the **fun** begins. Using colored chalk, begin to find all the new sentences you can find by drawing colored lines across the page and under any combination you choose. Try to find the most descriptive . . . the funniest, the craziest . . . the one that sparks your imagination the most . . . etc. Then use the one you like best to create your own new story. (See sample.)

This activity can be used over and over again with interesting sentences from your own writing or from the material you are reading. As you break the sentences down into parts you can begin to label the parts so that you can teach verbs, nouns, objects, etc.

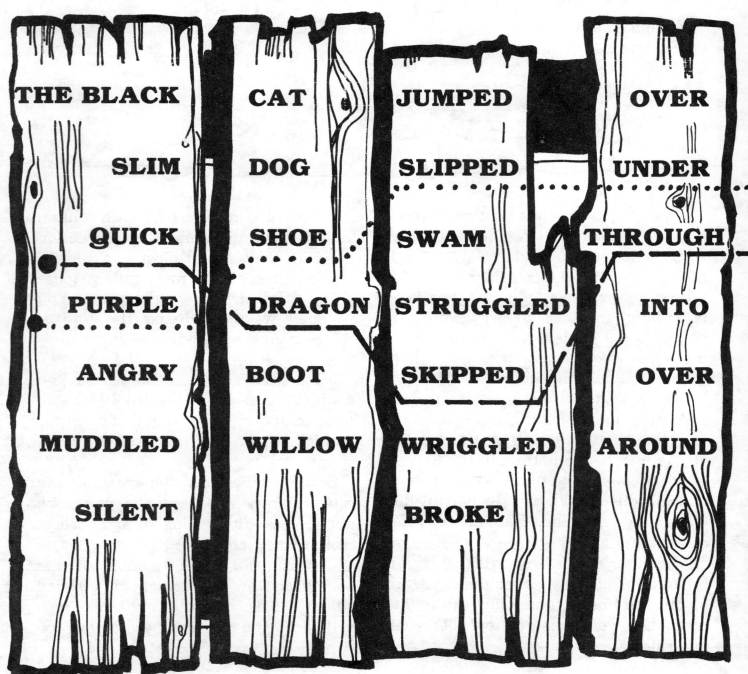

THE BLACK	CAT	JUMPED	OVER
SLIM	DOG	SLIPPED	UNDER
QUICK	SHOE	SWAM	THROUGH
PURPLE	DRAGON	STRUGGLED	INTO
ANGRY	BOOT	SKIPPED	OVER
MUDDLED	WILLOW	WRIGGLED	AROUND
SILENT		BROKE	

THE FENCE

THE WALL

THE HOLE

THE BAG

THE SPIRE

THE HILL

AND RAN AWAY

AND DISAPPEARED

AND CRIED

AND DIED

AND LAUGHED

AND HID
QUIETLY

First you will need several hats or buckets. Write each of the words in each of the following word groups on a card and place the cards in a hat or a bucket. Identify each group by putting the words on cards of the same color and putting them in a container of that color. Get your students into trios. Their task is to take one of the buckets and as quickly as they can to put **all** the words in it together into **one** long sentence. They may add other words; they may change endings, tense or form of the words as long as the root is there. Give them 15 minutes to see how many different sentences they can come up with.

Once this is done, they are to pick one of their sentences and refine it into one sentence they like very much and use it as the beginning of a story they are going to write together.

The next time they do this they will be using a different bucket and a different set of words.

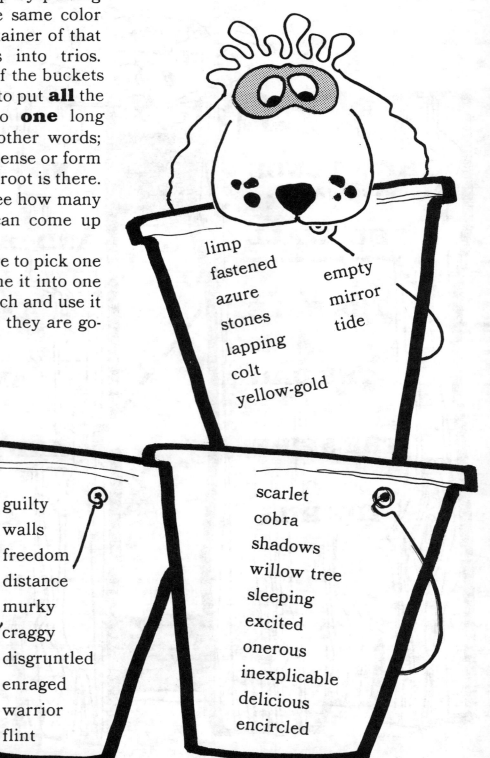

limp
fastened
azure
stones
lapping
colt
yellow-gold
empty
mirror
tide

guilty
walls
freedom
distance
murky
craggy
disgruntled
enraged
warrior
flint

scarlet
cobra
shadows
willow tree
sleeping
excited
onerous
inexplicable
delicious
encircled

particular
orange
rotund
leathery
simple

tower
singular
luscious
moon
adroit

bound
anchored
flexible
wrapped
stink
plausible

dawning
slippery
jacket
ragged

broken
quickly
twisted
exhilarating
swollen
cascading
softly
brazen
exceptional
despicable

pomegranate
filmy
desolate
rugged
wild
crackling
scattered
wrinkled
velvet
ancient

dandelion
watermelon
embers
lemonade
silky
waterfall
tangled
teardrops
feline
stallion

cultivated
friends
mechanical
robotics
reasonable
tender
aroma
disgusted
plentiful
determined

(3)

A variation of this activity is to place one of the buckets in front of the class. At a signal one trio comes up and as quickly as they can, they are to arrange the words in the tray under the chalkboard in an order. A second trio is then to put them into a sentence **in that same order** by adding any other words they need to create a complete sentence. For example, the following order—stallion, lemonade, silky, waterfall, tangled, embers, dandelion, feline—might become the following sentence: **A young stallion, the color of lemonade, stood near the silky waterfall which swept downstream near the tangled ruins and embers of a village where Dandelion the feline had lived in years past**.

(4)

Get your students into trios. Introduce this idea by talking about excuses. What are some they have used for being late, not doing a chore, getting into some kind of trouble. Now, one of the partners is to describe a situation where he had to make an excuse. Then they are to brainstorm at least five different excuses that might have worked better. Number two will then describe a new situation, and they will again brainstorm excuses. Now, **switch** partners and do it again. How many different ways can they think of to excuse themselves?

(5)

This activity will help students think about emotional content of their words. Get students into groups of five or six. Secretly give each one of them an emotion which has been printed on a card. Tell your students not to let anyone know what emotions they have. When you say "Begin," the first student is to recite "Mary Had a Little Lamb," trying to put his emotion into the poem. It is the task of his partner to try to decide which emotion he is trying to convey. Try this with as many different emotions as possible with the same poem.

(6)

How many ways can you get out of something. In the center of a group, place a stack of cards with the following written on them . . . plus many more of your own:

prison cell	locked car
elevator	boat with no oars
trap	up a tree
inside a box	under a log
closet	bank vault
basement	cave
attic	deep woods

One at a time a card is turned over and each student takes a turn at showing **nonverbally** one way to try to escape from that place. When all of them have shown a way, they are to talk about what they saw each other do and how well the idea was communicated.

USING YOUR HEAD

Coordinate with:

Social studies
Self-concept
Emotions
History
Famous people
Storytelling
Literature

⑦ The motivation for this activity is simply wonderful and can result in an on-going exploration of self-concept and feelings as well as language arts development and creativity. To introduce this to your class, have each bring an empty box to school. It must be the size of a bread box or smaller. Explain that they can bring anything from a matchbox to a shoe box to a corregated carton.

Explain to them that in order to get some ideas we are going to brainstorm all the kinds of boxes we can think of. Then we will have some ideas from which to choose if we wish. As they call out kinds of boxes, write them on the board . . . get some help if you wish and two or three of you write at the board while the rest of the class calls out boxes. To get you started you may wish to suggest things like:

shoe box	suit box	spice box
hatbox	flower box	milk carton
cereal box	toothbrush box	egg carton
matchbox	cassette tape box	
oatmeal box	shirt box	

This will help students think of different sizes, shapes and materials. It may take several days for everyone to get a box to the classroom; but when they all have one, you will be ready to begin.

There are many different activities to do with these wonderful box heads.

(8)

Give your class the following instructions: you are to take your box and make it into a three-dimensional self-portrait. It should end up looking as much like you as you can make it. You can use any materials you wish: paper, yarn, paint, cloth, rickrack, buttons, etc. But make that box look like **your head**. There is one restriction. When you are finished, it must still be able to be opened without destroying the face or head in any way. You may want to take a class period or two for working on their box portraits and perhaps give students a day or two to think about them before you start.

(9)

Have students put them all into a large pile and over the lunch hour mix them up a bit. When the students return have them pick up a box at random. Then, when they all have a box . . . they need to try to decide to whom it belongs. (I hope you have made one for yourself so that you can participate as well.) You can do this three or four different times. Each time the students will pick a different head and try to identify its owner.

(10)

Place a table against a wall and stack the heads against the wall on the table. You may have to use some tape or pins to hold them in place. This will create a wall "collage" of heads . . . all stacked up together. Label the table **all about us** and string yarn from each box to a place on the table where you will have an object important to that child or a poem, picture or story written by that student.

(11)

Get three classes to do this project simultaneously. Then when they are completed, take the classes to the gym and see if they can match the other classes to their box portraits.

What did you find out about someone
else that surprised you?

What did you find out that was
similar to yourself?

Did you enjoy finding out more about
someone?

Do we sometimes make judgements
about others before we really know
enough about them? Can you share
an example that happened with one
of your partners in this activity?

Do you think people are more simple
or more complex than you had
previously thought?

⑬

About once a week have students
bring something different to class in
their "heads." Some possibilities could
be:

Bring something that represents a
feeling you have had about something in the last week.

Bring something that represents
something about an important person in your life.

Bring something that represents
something you believe no one else
knows about you. (This should be
something you are willing to share
with the class.)

⑫

A wonderful sharing activity in the
classroom begins when all have completed their heads. Invite them to take
them home and place something (or
things) inside them that has an important meaning to them or represents an
important time in their lives. When
they bring them back, put them into
partners. Switch heads. Each person
looks inside partner's "head" and takes
out what he finds. He then tries to
figure out and verbally explain why he
thinks his partner put that particular
object into his head. Give them five to
ten minutes to talk about these objects;
then switch partners and do it again. Do
this several times. A large group discussion can then revolve around the following questions:

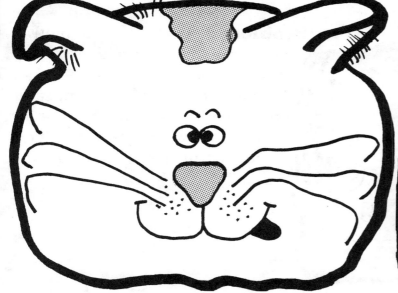

(14)

Have each student write a small paragraph that describes something about himself. Put all of these in a pile and line up the heads around the room. Invite each student to pick a paragraph at random (no names on them) and try to match it to the head of the person it talks about.

(15)

Each morning let three different students take the "heads" and group them into different categories. See over a two-week period how many different categories your students can think of for the "heads."

(16)

If the entire school makes these heads, a gigantic collage can be created for the front hall for special occasions when there will be guests in the building.

Each day take three different heads and place them together in front of the class. Put students in trios. Each trio is to give each head a fictitious name . . . and draw a body to go with the head. Then they will write a story starter using those three characters as the main characters in the story. Explain that a story starter should include:

1. a main character
2. a setting
3. a problem

You may wish to brainstorm settings and problems and list the ideas on the board in order to give students some ideas to start with. Some places to begin could be:

Setting (place)
    rainy midnight on the beach
    basement of an old castle
    crowded subway at 6 p.m.
    dirt road through a desert valley
    jet plane at 30,000 feet
    east tower of a haunted fortress

Problem (beginning of the plot)
    a hurricane is approaching
    noises in the attic
    four pair of shoes have disappeared
    a message was found pushed under
        the door which read: Watch out
        for the man in the orange knit
        hat.

Coordinate with:

Geology
Self-concept
Current events
Social studies
Career education

HOLES ARE FOR DIGGING

Write this on your board:
How much dirt is in a hole 3 feet wide, 5 feet deep and 9 feet long?

Answer: None, a hole is empty.

Ask your students:
How many of you have a hole in your sock? Then slyly reply, "No? Then how did you get your foot in?"

⑱

11

19

Put your students into groups of five. One will be the "recording secretary." Everyone is to brainstorm ideas while the secretary writes them down. What ideas? Well, what are all the kinds of holes you can think of? Encourage "jumping categories." For example: buttonholes, pit, canyon, ant hole, keyhole, knothole, mole hole, "I can't believe I ate the whole thing," cave, basement, bomb shelter, etc.

Now each group will put one of the holes in the middle of a large sheet of paper and create a web of ideas that surround and are suggested by the "hole" in the middle.

20

Each of these can now be a topic for a one-minute extemporaneous speech. First do these spontaneously in each group where students are addressing just the other four in the group. Then give students one week to research their topic and come back and do another one-minute speech using information and ideas they found in their research.

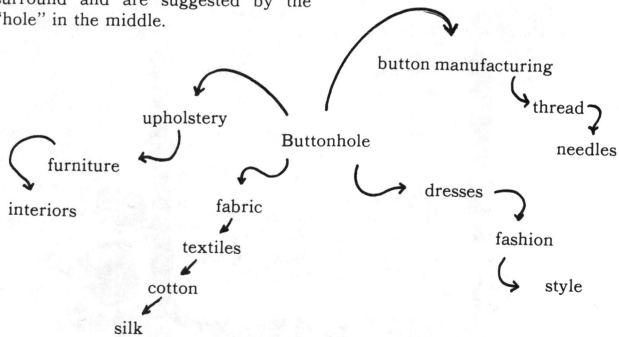

12

You will need a shovel and three to five garbage bags for this one. Students in groups of six go to each of six different places and dig **one** shovelful. Put the contents in the bag and bring it back to class. Before they go they should decide:

1. where to go
2. who will dig
3. who will carry the bag and shovel

They should also predict as closely as possible everything they think they will find in the "hole." Then when they return to the class, spread plastic on the floor, dump out their "hole" and list everything they can find. Have them list their findings, compare it to their predicted list, compare them with other groups, and finally categorize the findings. Have them decide what categories would be important to them as consumers. See if they can determine what categories might be important if they were any of the following:

Pest controller
Environmentalist
Anthropologist
Building contractor

Be sure your groups dig in some very different places: beach, school yard, empty lot, vegetable garden, near the foundation of a house, under a log in the woods, in the mud by a pond . . . .

(22)

Get your students into groups of three and have them brainstorm all the things that are **useless** because they get holes in them, and all the things that are **useful** because they **have** holes in them. Some examples of both might be:

cup   sink
dam   collander
sock   sieve
sweater   room (windows,
pan   doors)
balloon

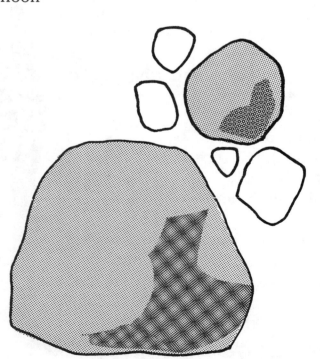

(23)

Put your students into partners and have them select a digging animal. Together they are to decide:

1. what they think is the single most important characteristic of that animal that equips it for digging.
2. what method it uses for digging.
3. why it digs (dwelling? food? protection?).

Then they are to find out how and why that animal digs and present the animal in some medium in **3-dimension** to the rest of the class. The presentation should show clearly how that animal digs.

(24)

Get with a partner. First list all the things that would be different if human beings lived in holes in the ground. Then draw a "blueprint" for the "hole-in-the-ground" home you would most like to live in. Consider such things as:

rain   cold
ventilation   storage
heat   energy

(Before you do the activity on the preceding page, go to a lumber or hardware store and find a book on underground homes. Tack some of the diagrams on the bulletin board and discuss why they are built as they are. This will better enable your students to talk and think about underground living.)

㉕ Invite an "oil man or woman" to class to share how an oil well is dug. If possible have him bring samples of the "core" that is retained as the well is dug. Have students in partners generate at least three questions to ask this person while he is with your class. After he has gone, hold your discussion and then have each pair of partners think of all the jobs that people do that require "digging." Be sure to encourage them to think of many kinds of digging, not just digging in the ground. Some professions they might think of:

Architect
Tunnel construction
Oil exploration
Coal miner
Farmer
Landscape designer
Sand and gravel company
Researcher (digging for information)
Lawyer (digging for evidence)
Dentist (digging ?)

㉖ List on the board all the animals your class can think of that live in or dig holes:

woodpecker	muskrat	gopher
clam	beaver	lion
mole	mud wasp	termite
ant	worm	

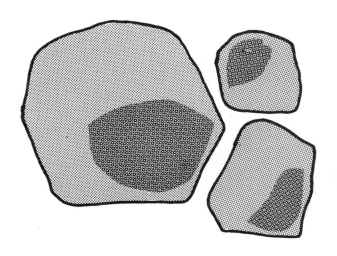

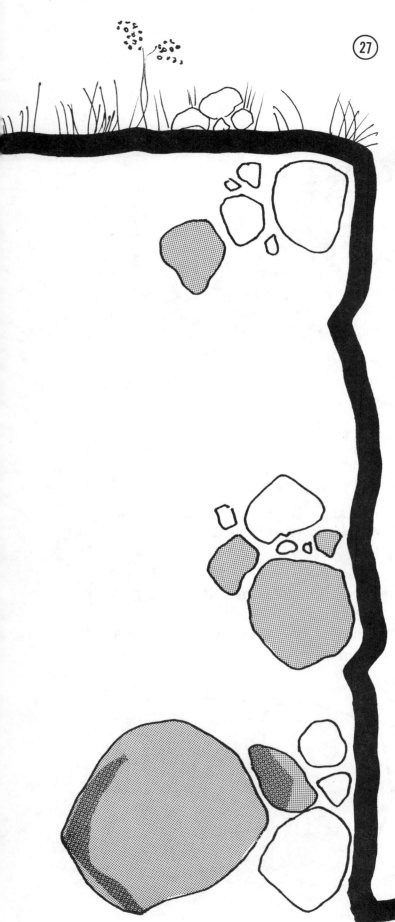

Get your students on their feet in the middle of the room. Clear everything away and explain that you are going to ask some forced choices. They must make a decision in each of the choices. They make their choices by moving to one side of the room or the other.

Would you rather be a coal miner or a window washer? (Designate one side of the room for the miner, the other for the washer.)

When students have chosen, ask some of them to tell why they made their choices. Then try some of the following and have students generate some of their own. (This can be done with many different content areas.)

Which would you be, a construction worker or a dentist?

Which would you choose, being a termite or a mole?

Would you be the Grand Canyon or a bombshelter?

Would you dig with a shovel or a spoon?

Would you rather be a lawyer or a doctor?

Would you rather be a forest ranger or an accountant in a large city?

BE A YO·YO

Coordinate with:

Tools
Home economics
Weather
Geography
Science
Botany

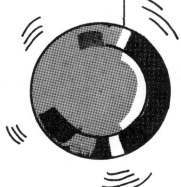

It is O.K. to be a yo-yo once in a while! This activity acts as a motivation to spark imagination and visual thinking. First use it several times by itself; then begin to use it in relation to any story or poem your class is reading or writing.

Get your class into partners. Face each other. Sit so that one of you can see the screen and one of you cannot see the screen. (Remember, however, that partners must be facing each other.) When I show you a word (a noun, name of an object), the person facing the screen is to let his partner know what the object is. He does **not** tell him, and he does **not** use the object. Instead he lets his **whole** body become the object. Give them about 5 seconds for each one. Each time the partner is to try to guess, out loud, what his partner has become. After 5 to 10 seconds, call it out so that everyone hears it and go on to the next one. One partner is becoming the objects, the other is guessing what they are. This is lots of fun and gets the imagination going. Several lists follow that you can begin with. After you have done these (tell the guessers what the category is; they will be more successful), begin creating your own lists from stories, poems, and other content you may be reading or studying. This is also a great way to introduce new vocabulary words.

Also note that in specific content areas you may allow **both** partners to see the screen. This gives the guesser the opportunity to make choices from among possibilities, and they will be more successful.

WEATHER
tornado
hurricane
cloud forming
raindrop falling
puddle forming
breeze
gust of wind
blast of Arctic air
sun rising

TOYS
yo-yo
rattle
race car
top
robot
teddy bear
baby doll

TOOLS
scissors
pencil sharpener
pliers
crescent wrench
saw
needle
clippers
shovel

BOTANY
grass growing up
flower unfolding,
  wilting, dying
leaves dropping, blowing,
  getting stuck in a
  corner
willow bending in wind . . .
first gentle, strong,
  torrential

KITCHEN
pop-up toaster
mixer
coffee maker
grater
salad fork and spoon
eggbeater
can opener

SCIENCE
(for two or more students)
Cell growing and dividing
Amoeba eating another cell
Hydrogen and oxygen molecules join-
  ing to become water
Water molecules heating up and
  becoming steam
Water molecules cooling down and
  becoming ice
Light reflecting from a mirror at
  many different angles

GEOGRAPHY
stream
mountain eroding
waves on a beach . . . calm
waves on a beach . . . strong
Mississippi flood plain
rapids
volcano erupting (small)
volcano erupting (disaster)
hailstones hitting concrete

(29)

Get a partner and sit facing each other. One partner holds his hands up loosely and in a relaxed manner in front of him. Explain to the class that this partner's hands just turned into Silly Putty. Silly Putty cannot do anything by itself, but if a sculptor (the other partner) "sculpts" those two hands, that sculptor can sculpt those two hands into anything he desires. Remember . . . Silly Putty will stay in any shape into which it is molded, but it won't do anything by itself. So . . . first partner, sculpt both of your partner's (#2) hands into (alternate partners sculpting with each item):

> a large capital "W"
> an "S"
> a teapot
> a baby buggy
> an eagle in flight
> a swan floating quietly
> a frog about to hop
> a butterfly
> a spider on a web

(30)

This time Partner #1 may use both **hands** and the **arms** of Partner #2. Try the following and alternate each time:

> a cash register
> a dying flower
> a snake in the grass
> an iron gate

(31)

This time Partner #1 may use the entire body of his partner to sculpt the object. Again alternate being the sculptor:

> a hat rack
> a toadstool
> a bridge
> a sports car
> a sailboat

(32)

The final stage in this series is to put students into groups of six. One person will be the sculptor and this person will sculpt all of the "team" together into something. The first time through, these will be "still" or "frozen" scenes. The second time through and on a signal, the scene can move and have sound. Try out the following to get you started:

> a carousel
> a crowded subway train
> a crowd at an amusement park
> tourists at the Statue of Liberty
> a storm gathering, storming and dying
> a supermarket on the Saturday before July 4th.

Once you have used this entire sequence and your students can handle the experiences, you can use any stage at any time depending on what you wish them to do. From here on, try taking things from your content whenever you want to wake them up, trigger the imagination and/or develop visual-spatial thinking. It also increases recall and comprehension of content. And **kids love it!**

Coordinate with:

Character development
Literature
English
History
Social studies

THE PLOT THICKENS

㉝

What are the elements of a good story? How do you convey this to students in an exciting and motivating manner? This unit takes a bit of preparation but will teach the basic elements of plot and help students write more interesting stories.

First you will need six sheets of colored construction paper with the designs on the following page cut out and pasted on as shown.

Be sure that the circles are always the same color, the squares the same color, etc. This is shown with patterns in the example. If you look closely at the example, you will see that in sequence the six sheets can be interpreted as a famous nursery rhyme. Can you figure out which one is shown in the example? It is "Humpty Dumpty." Almost every nursery rhyme and fairy tale follows the same pattern, and it is a basic plot line that can be used for all kinds of storytelling.

Now, go back and again look at the six pages in sequence.

Page 1

Main character with a hint of description.

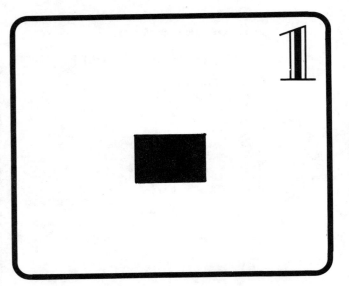

Page 2

Main character **doing** something.

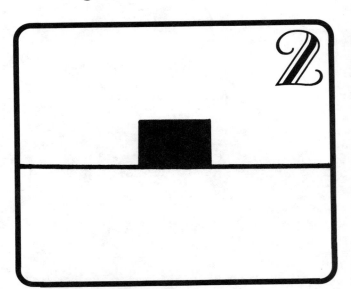

Page 4

Enter the adversary or protagonist.

Page 3
Main character with added
action or change in the action.

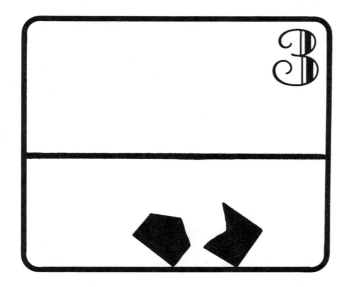

First, make several sets of six-page
stories based on nursery rhymes. Show
them to your class and see if they can
figure them out. Some good ones could
be "Little Red Riding Hood," "Little
Miss Muffet," "Goldilocks," "Snow
White." Notice that the shapes that
represent the characters are **symbolic**; they are not representational.
("Snow White" might be a green
square). This is intentional. This will
encourage students to visualize in their
own manner.

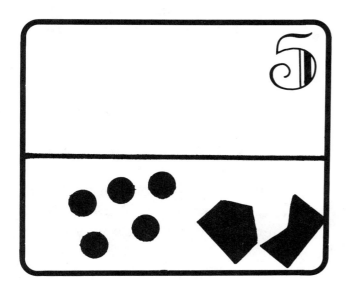

Page 5
Protagonist does something
that creates a problem.

Page 6
Main character interacts with
protagonist to resolve the
problem.

(34)

After students have looked at three or four of these, figured them out and gotten the idea, put them into trios with scissors, colored paper and glue. Each group is to pick a nursery rhyme or fairy tale they think **no one else in the room is going to choose** and turn it into a six-page symbolic story. When this is done, each day put a different one in front of the class and see if the class can figure out the story.

(35)

Now they are ready to create their own **new** fairy tale. Use "Humpty Dumpty" or "Little Miss Muffet" as a model. Put your students into trios. Hold up page one and tell your students they are to create a main character. (See "Tip Your Hat," page 42 of **Breaking Language Barriers**.) When that is done, move to page two where they give the main character an action . . . and so on through the six pages. The first time this is done they are to match each page with **one written line only**. They will end up with a very simple six-line story, but with all the elements of a basic plot. Share these simple stories with each other.

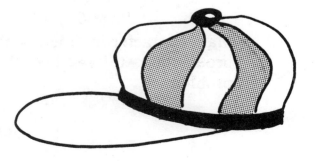

(36)

Second time around, each page should represent a paragraph . . . at least three sentences. Page one for example would be a paragraph introducing the main character and describing him. Now your effort will result in a six-paragraph story. (Work on paragraph development while you do this one.)

(37)

The third time around each visual page of the nursery rhyme will represent **three** paragraphs. Now you have expanded your story to eighteen paragraphs.

(38)

After trios have created their stories at any of the above three levels, an exciting task is to put two trios together . . . . Have them share their stories with each other, then figure out a way to put the stories together to make one story. When you do this tell your students:

- One of the main characters must now become a supporting character.
- You should end up with a main plot and a subplot.
- The story can be much longer because it has much more interesting action.

boxed in

The motivation for this unit is similar to another unit in this book, but we will go in a brand-new direction with it. Have each student bring a **box** to class—any size, shape, color. You may want to restrict it to a size that one person can carry . . . easily. Once you have all the boxes, line them up across the front of the room . . . or display them all on a table . . . then . . .

Coordinate with:

Career education
Consumer education
Home economics
Feelings
Vocabulary development
Self-image

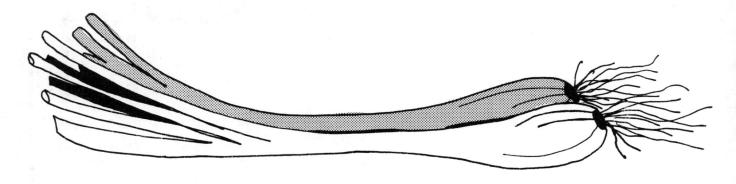

(39) Everyone get comfortable; we are going on a short trip in our imaginations. Lie down on the floor . . . breathe deeply and just imagine this . . .

You are sitting on a shelf at the supermarket . . . . You are sitting there in the dark with hundreds of other boxes . . . . You are closely packed on the shelf with boxes just like yourself . . . . You all look alike . . . . You all feel alike . . . . You are the same shape, the same color . . . and you are stuffed full of raw oatmeal. You feel about to burst . . . . The store is dark and silent . . . . It is 7 a.m. on a Saturday morning and soon you know the lights will come on and you will wait . . . . You are sitting on the front row . . . . Today you may begin your incredible journey . . . suddenly the lights flicker on . . . you can hear noises, voices and clerks seem to be bustling around . . . getting ready for the morning rush. The doors have been opened . . . and now you hear the soft shir, shir . . . shir . . . of the wheels of grocery carts . . . . A woman goes by in a hurry and then another. They don't even glance in your direction. Several more pass by . . . . Here is one who is strolling . . . looking along the shelves . . . she has stopped in front of you . . . she is looking straight at you and reaching out toward you . . . . Her arm is covered with bracelets that jingle and jangle . . . her nails are long and red . . . she **grabs** the box next to you . . . shakes it and dumps it into her cart . . . then she quickly walks away. Now men, women . . . boys and girls . . . all kinds of people are going by . . . . girls in T-shirts, fathers with sons crowding the aisles . . . little old blue-haired ladies . . . . The aisles are crowded with shoppers . . . and still you sit . . . waiting . . . waiting . . . . A woman in a long yellow

coat comes into view . . . a baby in her cart . . . . She stops in front of you
. . . . Without looking for more than a second, she grabs you roughly
around the middle . . . shakes you till your brains rattle and carelessly
tosses you into the cart. You tumble and bounce on top of a bag of
oranges and land upside down near the pickles. Your insides are head-
over-heels . . . . You feel sick at your stomach . . . . And the woman in the
yellow coat wheels you quickly down the aisle and into the nearest
checkout stand . . . . Again you are grabbed, pushed, slid across the
counter, yanked up by one end, and plop, find yourself sitting in the
dark in the bottom of a brown paper bag. Suddenly a wet chicken lands
on your head, three onions and a turnip tumble down beside you . . .
four boxes of Kleenex block out all the light . . . and you find yourself
waiting again. You seem to be moving, lifted . . . carried . . . and then left
alone . . . sitting somewhere . . . soon the chicken and tissues are lifted
up and away . . . . Light floods in as you are lifted and placed on a bright
yellow countertop . . . . A fingernail pokes under your top and pops up
your flap. Fingers tear away your top and riiiiiiiiiiiip open your inner
bag. You are turned roughly upside down . . . again . . . and all your oats
go spinning and falling away into a glass container . . . . You are being
held over a kitchen trash barrel . . . . You drop . . . down . . . down . . . into the bottom of the trash . . . the lid slams shut . . . leaving you in the
pitch, black darkness . . . so quickly your usefulness and adventure are
over . . . or are they????

Open your eyes and sit up when you are ready.

27

Get your students into trios. Ask them to describe to each other what they could see from their position on the grocery shelf. Ask them to first:

Describe the woman with the bracelets... then, as a group paint a picture of her. As a group they will need to agree on what she looked like and what she was wearing. Then they should decide on her personality, what kind of house she lives in and what she does for a living.

(41)

In your group have students discuss feelings they might have had while being ripped open and emptied. Ask them to think of three real-life situations that give them those same feelings. Then in a large group discussion, share some of those experiences and feelings.

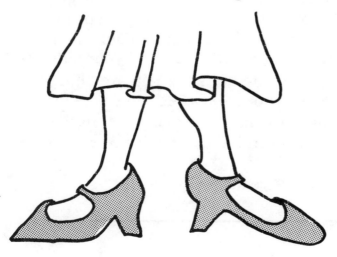

(42) In trios talk about the ending of this imaginary trip? Is it really over? Can the box in the story still be useful? Is its life over? Where will it go from here .... Instruct your students to write a new guided fantasy story that begins in the following way:

"You are an empty oatmeal box, and you just landed in the bottom of the trash can in the kitchen. Only moments ago the lid clanged shut and left you in the dark ... you can hear the owner's baby crying somewhere in the kitchen. You hope you don't have to stay in this dark can for too long .... Suddenly ..."

(43)

Now get students into trios and give each group a box. Give them one minute to list everything they can think of that:

1. might come in that box when it was new.
2. might be stored in it to keep it clean.
3. might be hidden in it to keep it a secret.

Have students recall things they received at some time in their lives that came in boxes and describe the objects and the events to their partners. Ask them to list any emotions they can recall that they felt when they received the boxes:

1. emotions they felt before they opened them.
2. emotions they felt while opening them.
3. emotions they felt after opening them.

Have each student find a space where he won't invade anyone else's space. Give the following directions: In a moment you are going to imagine being inside a small space . . . a box. When I put you into that box, silently begin to explore the inside of it. It will change, and as I change it you continue to explore . . . nonverbally . . . the space in which you find yourself.

You are inside a large cardboard box . . . not quite high enough for you to stand up in and just a bit wider than your two arms outstretched . . . . It just changed into a tall refrigerator box . . . . Now it is a gigantic round box . . . now it is a telephone booth . . . now it is a closet . . . now it is a stone cell in a cellar . . . . Now it is a long narrow hallway . . . with some pictures on the wall . . . . One of them is very peculiar . . . . Examine it very carefully . . . . Now you are in a dark cave that gets smaller as you go deeper into it . . . feel the walls, hear the sounds . . . . Now it is the attic in a deserted house . . . . Now it is a box again and it is getting smaller . . . and smaller . . . and smaller . . . . It is getting so small you have to crouch . . . smaller . . . smaller . . . smaller . . . . You can't even move . . . . Freeze. Relax.

Now invite students to share some of the following with a neighbor:

Which space did you like best? least?
Which was the most vivid in your imagination?
What was so unusual about the image in the hall?
Describe some of the things you found in the closet . . . the cave . . . the hallway . . . .

(45)

Everyone find a space. When I say "Begin," you are going to imagine you are inside a box. Begin to explore the inside of the box. Decide on its size. Once you have established that, you will notice that the inside surface begins to change . . . . Begin . . . . The inside of that box just changed into sandpaper . . . splintery wood . . . velvet . . . cooked noodles . . . rough burlap . . . jam . . . marshmallows . . . ice . . . red hot metal . . . bricks . . . stones and mortar. . . tile . . . freeze and relax. Now, sit down with a neighbor. Recall all the surfaces you can and make at least three lists describing those surfaces. You have ten minutes to do this.

(46)

Get students into partners and give them a box. Have them think of five things they would like to cover the inside surfaces of the box with. Have them actually do this. Then pass the boxes around letting class members feel the surfaces as they write down words they can think of to describe those surfaces. As they do this have them drop the words into the boxes . . . then pass them on. Each group reads the words already in the box and adds two or three more.

(47)

Get your students into trios and give each group a box. Have them fill their box with something that can be shared with the class that costs **nothing**. Each Monday and Friday have a different group share what they put in their box with the class. Some possibilities might include wildflowers, a rock collection, photos of their family, their favorite toy, several fun poems, a book, a short story, a news article about someone they know, their favorite record, etc.

Get into partners. Give each pair a box. Their job is to decorate the outside of their box to look like their interpretation of a specific emotion. Give them a card with an emotion written on it. They are not to tell anyone their emotion. When all the boxes are finished, see if the class can tell what emotion each one represents. Some possibilities could include:

anger	anxiety
hate	disgust
fear	disappointment
joy	anticipation
pleasure	excitement
jealousy	sorrow
loneliness	pain
envy	horror
boredom	ecstasy
fascination	sadness

Discuss:

1. Why did the creators of a particular box use certain colors?
2. Do those colors mean the same thing to you as they did to the persons who created that box?
3. How were the colors on your box misinterpreted? Are your own personal feelings ever misinterpreted by others?
4. How do you let others know how you are feeling?
   List negative ways.
   List positive ways.
5. Just as wrappings hide the contents of a box, what feelings do you sometimes hide and how do you try to hide them? Are you successful? With whom?

Coordinate with:

Nutrition
Health
Plants, seeds
Plant reproduction
Vocabulary extension
Career education

IT'S THE PITS!

The motivation for this one is so simple and so much fun you won't be able to resist it. First, you will need a large piece of plastic or even two or three large plastic tablecloths. Spread out on the floor in the middle of the room before the students come back from lunch and place two large watermelons in the middle of the floor. When they come back, have them sit in a circle around the melons. Two students get at the board and write responses while the rest of the class rolls one melon around the circle. The person moving the melon calls out one word that describes the melon. Suggest to your students

Alternate partners, one at a time, completing the following sentence starters. Let each partner do each starter at least three different ways:

I bent over and tried to pick up the watermelon, but as I tried to get it into my arms, it suddenly _____ and then it _____.

The melon broke with a splat just as

_____

_____.

that they consider such things as color, taste, texture, smell, sounds, etc. When this is done, brainstorm one or more of the following:

1. What are all the ways to open this melon without a knife?
2. If you could find something inside this melon besides watermelon, what would it be?
3. What are all the things you could think of that might be made with a watermelon flavor?
4. Think up a new name for a watermelon? What should it be?

I opened my mouth as wide as I could and dove into that bright, juicy melon. My teeth suddenly felt _____, and my mouth felt like it was going to

_____

_____.

I ate so much watermelon my _____

_____.

When my dad saw what happened to my white shirt/blouse, he turned as red as watermelon and said, "_____

_____."

I was just about to take a big, juicy bite of my melon when it suddenly said, "_____,

and furthermore, _____."

The truckload of watermelons hit the curve doing just over 40 miles an hour. The driver felt his load shift and suddenly the truck was out of control careening over the curb and into _____

_____.

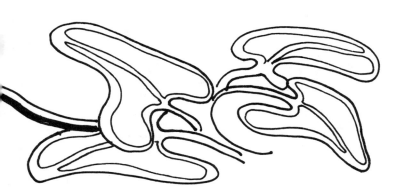

33

Of course, the only thing to do now is to get out a large knife, cut the melon . . . all the time listening carefully, smelling and, of course, anticipating the eating. When each student has a slice of melon, he must spend one full minute looking at it very closely observing everything he can. At the end of that time have students share something they hadn't noticed about watermelon before. Ask them to smell it slowly with their eyes closed and then describe to a partner a memory that comes to them about watermelon.

Now, very carefully, quietly and with a great deal of concentration, let everyone, slowly and with great relish, **eat** his slice of watermelon.

Have the students eat their melon over large pieces of drawing or sketch paper. Let their drippings dry as is . . . seeds and all. When they are dry, each student's task will be to write a poem on that page . . . but in and around the drippings from the watermelon stains. Let the stains dictate how students will organize their poems.

Now, get into partners. Partner number one begins to describe how to eat a watermelon in as much detail as possible . . . when you say "Switch," partner number two goes on with the description. Switch them back and forth as they are going to eat the melon. (All pairs of partners are doing this at the same time.)

Now, do the same thing again only uncover the following list of words that have been written on the board and encourage them to use as many of the words displayed as they can.

wet	dribble
runny	sloppy
squishy	icy
sweet	crisp
delicious	crimson
pungent	pink
refreshing	snappy
tart	scrumptious

Go to a large nursery and explain that you are working with a classroom and ask to borrow some samples of dried seedpods. Florists use them in all kinds of dried arrangements. Gather many samples of seedpods from your neighborhood and town. Have students bring as many kinds as they can find. Place the collection on a table and arrange them. On a second table arrange some of the following: orange, apple, grapefruit, banana, pomegranate. Look at both tables.

1. What do the objects on both tables have in common?
2. How many ways can you see that seeds are transported?
3. Why do you think some plants produce large seeds, tiny seeds? Some produce many seeds and others just a few?

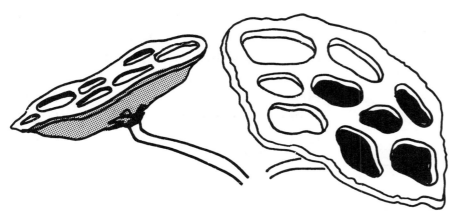

Give each student a seedpod to work with . . . water lily pods are wonderful for this. With a soft pencil and paper, have them draw the pods as carefully as they can. The design in the pod itself is quite beautiful. Have each student, using the pod as a motivation, create an "organic" design and produce it in paint, or perhaps cut paper.

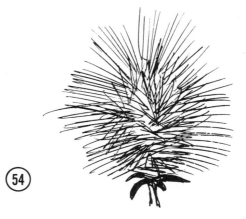

(54)

Any large grocery store will carry watermelon flavored candy. Buy enough for each student. As they suck on the candy have them write as many words as they can that describe that flavor. Repeat the same process with lemon drops and peppermint. Then create three lists at the front of the room that will look something like the following (only yours will be generated by your classroom).

LEMON DROP

    tart
    lemony
    puckery
    sour

WATERMELON

    sweet
    tangy
    tart
    smooth
    wonderful

PEPPERMINT

    bright
    sharp
    fresh
    alive

Now, write one sentence that has a word from each of the three columns. Try coming up with two or three sentences. Then:

Write a sentence about a cat that has a word from each column.

Write about your morning using one word from each column.

Write a sentence about falling asleep with at least one word from each column.

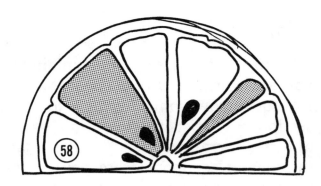

Take one word from each column, picking the most **unrelated** words you can find and try writing them into one sentence.

Write a paragraph about a storm with at least one word from each column.

What else could you write about using these words?

Ask your produce man for untreated avocados. Put your students into groups of five and have each group bring one avocado to class with them. In each group, pass the avocado around, smell it, feel it, brainstorm words about it and have one "recording secretary" write down the words in each group. Then, using a small paring knife cut the avocado in half, remove the seed, very carefully, and slice the avocado. Taste it and get reactions. How many like it? How many don't?

Take all the leftover avocados . . . place them in a bowl and add chopped onion, chopped canned tomatoes, a bit of Tabasco and mash it all together. Now let students all taste guacamole sauce. How do they feel about it? Like it? Don't like it?

See if you can find out the largest seed on earth and the smallest seed on earth.

Have each group of five support their avocado seed in water using toothpicks, place them near the windows . . . and write their closest estimate to when they believe they will see the first signs of it beginning to grow.

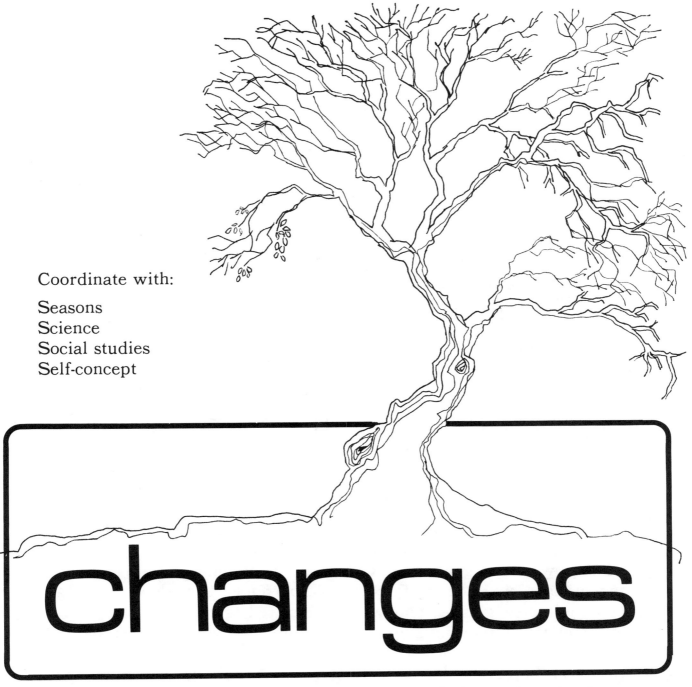

Coordinate with:

Seasons
Science
Social studies
Self-concept

changes

(61) Close your eyes. Relax. We are going on a trip in our imaginations. You are standing on a slight rise in the prairie of west Texas. You stand alone. Solitary. Singular against a bleak, gray and dreary landscape. It is winter and you are a mesquite tree. Evening is coming on and a chilly wind whistles through your frozen branches. They click together and crackle with fragments of ice and snow. As the darkness grows heavier, you see lights blink on in farmhouses out there in the darkness. You stand. You do not move. You barely feel the life within you. You have been resting. Your roots are deep in the frozen soil. Your sap is down and waiting for the first tentative touch of spring which you know will soon be coming. You have been sleeping in this icy, lonely and barren land.

The days drift by and you are only barely aware that they pass . . . but something is stirring in you . . . . The sun seems warmer, the ice fragments melt and fall away . . . the earth begins to thaw and small prairie creatures begin to stir about the base of your trunk . . . . The wind grows softer, gentler and warmer . . . . The snows turn to rain and as you look about you see the dry, cold barren earth is slowly turning green with new grasses. Tiny wildflowers are beginning to pop up . . . . You feel your sap pushing up . . . . Your branches grow warmer and as you push out tiny, new leaves, fresh, crisp green leaves on the tips of your arms pop out and begin to uncurl . . . . A robin lands on your arm and begins to sing. The sun warms you and as you look at a new day the prairie has come alive in wondrous carpets of lavender, pink and blue blossoms. The Texas wildflowers are, seemingly overnight, running in rampant color across the new red earth . . . . Color is bursting out all around you, and the air is alive with bees, birds and dragonflies who welcome spring with enthusiastic buzzing . . . . As you breathe deeply into the fresh new days, your leaves grow strong and the days gain hours . . . . The air is warmer, almost hot and the friendly, new sun of spring is quickly becoming the unforgiving sun of summer . . . . Thunderstorms gather and drop buckets of rain in torrents around you and lightning crackles at you across the open expanses . . . . Then the

storms move on . . . . The heat grows oppressive . . . . The air is still and hot . . . . The new earth turns to cracked, summer clay and dust rises in great gusts before the furnace of hot summer winds . . . . You choke and struggle for air . . . . Your leaves hang limp against a sinister sky and heat waves rise harshly from the starving earth . . . . As you stand in the stillness you feel the first light touch of cooler air . . . a breath from the north across the Dakotas, into Oklahoma . . . and down to you . . . . You are released from the intense heat and you quiver at the thought of fall . . . . The days are growing shorter now and the evenings have put on a chill . . . . The summer sky, no longer angry, is crisp, and blue, and cool . . . . The nights are colder, dipping down toward freezing . . . . You feel your leaves begin to loosen their hold as yellow creeps into their veins . . . . They turn slowly to crimson and gold and brown . . . . The air chills you to the core . . . . The small prairie animals scurry about in a great rush getting ready for winter . . . . And sure enough the night comes whistling in with a cold snap hard enough to hear . . . . It spreads over the land like an ice-cold hand, stilling the sap . . . driving the creatures into their dens . . . and turning the brown summer grasses to a cold, hard matted cover festooned with frost in the hours before dawn . . . . And then just before you fall into your winter sleep, the soft snow, like a white velvet shroud, covers the prairie and whispers, "Be still . . . , be silent . . . rest . . . I am winter . . . ." . . . and you sleep once more. Cold . . . . Frozen . . . . Still . . . in this lonely, barren land . . . . Relax . . . . When you are ready, open your eyes.

(63) Place a large leaf of some kind (get one from a florist) in a jar (no water) in front of your class. Get into partners. Each pair of partners will make a thirty-day calendar with large boxes. Each day they are to brainstorm ten words that describe the leaf and write them in the box for that day. The words can be the same as the day before if they are still appropriate. Watch to see how and when the words change; they will change as the leaf changes.

(64)

Do the above activity with many different things. Each pair of partners will have a different object to watch for thirty days and describe with ten words. Some of the objects to use can be:

a flower
an orange
a grape
a cooked hamburger patty
a rock
a glass of milk
a slice of bread
a caterpillar
a small growing plant
a silver spoon
a raw hamburger patty
a block of wood

(62)

In groups of three, discuss ice changing to water. What happens when ice melts? Have each trio pick a place to put an ice cube for the day. Then decide what to put it on: metal, wood, cloth. Also have one cube in a glass of water alone, another in water with other cubes, one in warm water, and one in cold water. Be sure to place one in the sun and one in the shade. Have your students predict the hour and minute when they think their ice cube will be melted . . . completely. Check your ice cubes every fifteen minutes and when the ice gets very small, watch it very closely. See how much time it took the ice cubes to melt. Make a class graph of the times. Compare them.

After you begin the above activity, put your students into trios and tell them they must reach "consensus" on at least three of the items being observed in the room. They should make a statement concerning the following:

1. How will it change and what will happen?
2. How fast will it change?
3. What determines whether or not the object changes?

Compare their predictions with reality.

Get your students into trios. On a large sheet of paper have them list all the things that change in a **predictable** manner. Some suggestions might be:

baby—child—adult—elder
fall—winter—spring—summer
day—night—day

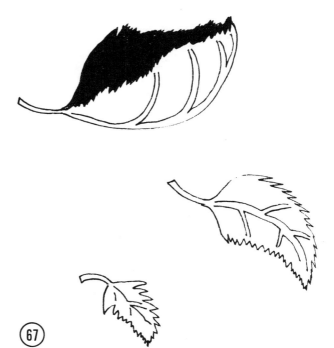

The following activity is excellent for self-image. In the first week of school, have every student make a hand and a footprint on a page with tempera paint. Give each a 6-foot piece of yarn in his favorite color and have him knot it at one end and put another knot at exactly how tall he is.

Now put these three things into a large envelope and put them away until January 12. Open the envelopes on January 12, make new hand and foot-prints, tie a third knot for the student's current height and notice the changes.

1. Were the students surprised?
2. Were the changes expected?
3. What other changes occurred?

Put these all back into the envelope a second time. As partners, have them make predictions for hand size, foot size and height for the last day of school. Repeat this process on the last day of school. Have there been significant changes in 9 months? How many?

Invite students to find pictures of their parents when they (the parents) were young and some pictures of them currently. Have them mounted on a board and compare them, then and now. The pictures will probably have a span of 18-25 years. What are all the things your students can observe that have changed? Have them, in small groups, list as many categories as they can. Some examples might be:

skirt lengths	house styles
makeup	automobiles
lapels	hair styles
the photos themselves	
colors and patterns	

70 From the above activity, get students into trios. Each trio will pick a topic and create a **visual** presentation of the changes that have taken place since 1900. Some possible categories could be:

cars	buildings
planes	roads
trains	women's roles
toys	dresses
houses	men's suits
hats	men's roles

When the presentations are displayed, be sure to play Jimmy Buffet's "Changes in Attitude, Changes in Latitude."

68 Put your students into groups of six. Have them sit in a circle. One person is blindfolded. Then five partners change chairs and mix up their order. Then, one at a time they sing "Happy Birthday" to the blindfolded student but in a **changed** or disguised voice. See how many of the singers the student can identify. This is excellent for listening and tonal recall. Let everyone have a chance to do this on his birthday. Or use it at other times and let students recite poems, etc. But always have a **changed** voice. How many ways can they think of to change their voices?

In partners have your students discuss, then decide: ⑦¹

1. If you could change **one** thing in the world, what would it be?
2. If you could add three abilities to yourself, what would they be?
3. If you could keep one thing the same forever what would it be?
4. Can you think of one thing that **never** changes?
5. What do you think is the most beautiful change you have ever seen? Describe it to your partner.
6. If you could change one group of people's attitudes about one thing, who and what would it be?
7. If you could change one thing in your past, what would it be?

⑦²

There is a wonderful song that goes: "To every season, turn, turn, turn. There is a reason, turn, turn, turn. A time for every purpose under heaven." Who did it? Why do you think they wrote it and what does it mean to you?

⑦³

This last activity takes some communication, some trust and some work. But it is excellent if you can work it out. Do this in the last half of the year when students are more likely to know each other and have friends in the classroom. This also depends upon parent involvement and consent. On a given day . . . when all permission slips and communications have been done, students will **change** families for a night. Students get into partners. They describe what an evening at home is like. Then each person goes to his partner's home for the evening. He eats dinner at his partner's home, does his homework, sleeps in his partner's bed, eat breakfast at his partner's and then comes back to school. As soon as class begins, put them together to discuss:

1. What did you find out about your partner?
2. What was different from your partner's description?
3. What surprised you?
4. How is your home and your partner's similar? different?

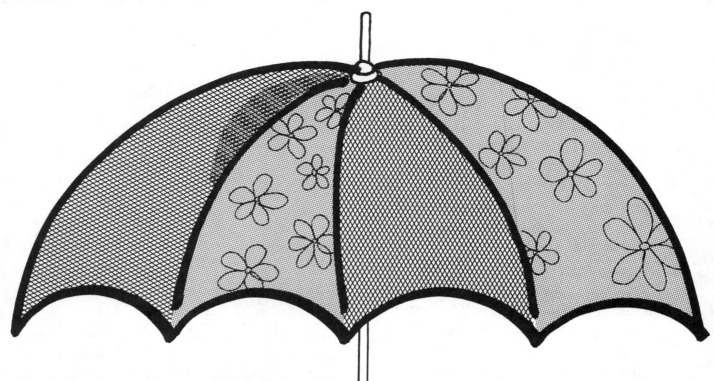

Of course, you must begin with a collection of umbrellas. Ask each student to bring one from home. Collect as many as you can. Stretch a cord across your room, as high as you can, and hang the open umbrellas from it by their handles. It will give your classroom instant excitement. Now you are ready for the following activities.

Coordinate with:

Weather
Storms
Water
Climate
Rivers and lakes

UMBRELLAS

Play the song "Rainy Days and Mondays" by the Carpenters and ask students to brainstorm all the reasons why rainy days "get them down." Ask each student to find a recording of at least one song about rainy days:

"Stormy Weather"
"Raindrops Keep Falling on My Head"
"Look for the Silver Lining"
"April Showers"

Listen to these songs and brainstorm two lists:

Negative About   Positive About

Rainy Days   Rainy Days

Your goal is to determine if there is as much beauty in a rainy day if you look for it as there is in a sunny day.

75

Hang an umbrella upside down from the middle of the room about three feet off the floor and fill it with cards with some of the following questions on them: (Add as many questions of your own as you choose. Be sure to keep them open-ended and interpretive.)

What would happen if raindrops were as large as watermelons?
What would happen if it rained every single day of the year except March 17?
What would happen if it really rained "cats and dogs"?
What would happen in your town if it rained torrentially for forty days and forty nights?
What if every raindrop that hit the ground caused a flower to grow on that spot?

How would you feel if you were suddenly inside a raindrop and falling from the sky?

What would happen if rain were purple and stained everything it touched?

What would happen if raindrops piled up like snow?

How is a raindrop like a snowflake?

How is getting caught in the rain like eating spaghetti?

How is a thundercloud like your brother or sister?

What would a single bolt of lightning flashing across the sky probably be saying?

How would you feel if you had grown up in the Sahara Desert and had never seen it rain, and you moved to a tropical island where it rained every day?

Hang an umbrella in the corner of the room, open, with the handle hanging down. From the tips of the ribs of the umbrella, hang strings of small cards. Let each card be the name of a book that is either about rain, or has a rainstorm in it . . . or can be related to rain, storms, or umbrellas. When a student reads one of these books, he puts his name on the back of the card and writes one word that describes the book for his classmates: great, wonderful, funny, sad, boring, tremendous, fair, etc. Down one side of the chalkboard, write a list of descriptions for students to make choices in case they can't think of one on their own.

From a hanging umbrella, hang blue, cut-out raindrops. On each raindrop print an **un-idea**. These are to be used when you think a student needs some quiet time. When John or Linda is "acting-out" you may say to them, "Go to the umbrella and select an un-idea and do it for the next fifteen minutes." Some ideas to get you going:

- Look out the window for five minutes and make a list of all the soft (or wrinkled, or wooden, or narrow) things you can see.

- Put your head down on your desk and dream about a happy time; then draw a picture of it in pastels.

- Listen to music on the headphones and cut out shapes that the music makes you think of. Glue these to a piece of paper in an interesting design.
- Go to the library and find a book about the rain.
- Draw something that happens only on a rainy day.
- Watch the clouds and try to see at least ten different images in them.

Get your students into partners. Give everyone a large sheet of watercolor paper. Each student will paint a sky . . . all over the entire sheet of paper. Use lots of water and lots of paint. Make it angry, or soft, or stormy, or clear . . . but make it interesting. Then let them all dry. When they are dry, exchange your sky with your partner. Look at your partner's sky and over it, in black, paint a silhouette of what you might see against that sky. Use only black and make it solid.

(78)

Divide into partners and alternately each student begins to draw something that is seen on a rainy day or in any kind of a storm. The student's partner tries to see how quickly he can identify what his partner is drawing. See how many different images the two partners can identify in five minutes.

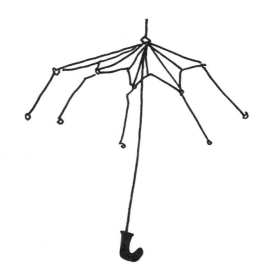

(79)

Take the covering off of an umbrella so that all you have left is the skeleton. Bring it into your classroom and "open" it up. Explain that this is a magical umbrella; and that if you could see the fabric, you would see that it is the most beautiful fabric in the world. Give students large sheets of paper with the outline as shown. They are to create the most beautiful designs for the umbrella that they can think of. Then cut them all out and create a wall mural with them.

(80)

Put your students into partners. The first partner tells a very short story of two to three sentences to his partner. An example might be: After dinner I heard the cat crying, so I filled her bowl with cat food, went out through the screen door to the porch and fed the poor thing. The second partner then retells the story, but adds as much color as possible: After dinner I heard my orange and black cat crying the blues, so I filled her yellow bowl with cat food, went out through the old green screen door to the faded gray porch and fed the poor thing.

This can be done with any idea or theme. The idea is to **think color**.

Have students first do two or three about an event on a **sunny** day. Then have them do two or three about an event on a **rainy** day. Now they can pick the one they like best and expand it into a paragraph or a story.

(81)

Divide your class into groups of five or six. Hold up one of your umbrellas. Say to your class: "We have the job of improving this umbrella. We have to make it better, or prettier, or more useful. Or we have to make it more fun to use or more interesting to use. There are many ways to do this. Let's see how many ideas you can come up with." Then give your class each of the following ideas and let them work on it for a few minutes:

Make it, or some part of it, bigger.
Make it, or some part of it, smaller.
Change what it is made of.
Reverse part or parts of it.
Add something to it.
Change the material it is made of.
Make parts of it automatic.
Add sound to it.
Add electricity to it.
Add another function to it in some way.

(82)

When all of these ideas have been listed and many of them shared, each group is to pick **one** idea from each of the above ideas and incorporate all of them into **one** umbrella and do a diagram, drawing and/or set of instructions for their **all new wonderful umbrella**.

(83)

Get into partners. Each partner, in turn, acts out a problem with an umbrella by actually getting up and doing it . . . nonverbally. His partner is to try to guess the problem. Then the second partner does the same thing, but with a new problem. In five minutes they are to try to come up with and identify as many problems with an umbrella as they can think of.

(84)

Give everyone three sheets of paper. Label one sheet "umbrella," the second "thundercloud" and the third "willow in the wind." When you say "Begin," they all begin to draw a picture of the object as labeled on a page . . . then you begin to call out page numbers. Page one! Page three! Page one! Page two! Call them out at random. Students are to move at random from page to page drawing three different things.

(85)

From your collection of umbrellas, take one each day and put it in the closet. Let students see if they are observant enough to determine which umbrella (or umbrellas) is missing!

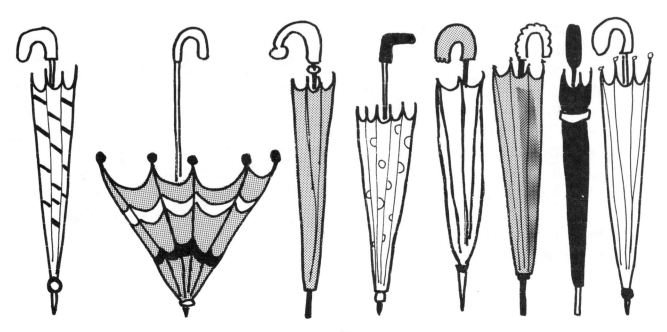

Coordinate with:

Transportation
Travel
History
American history
Social studies
Countries

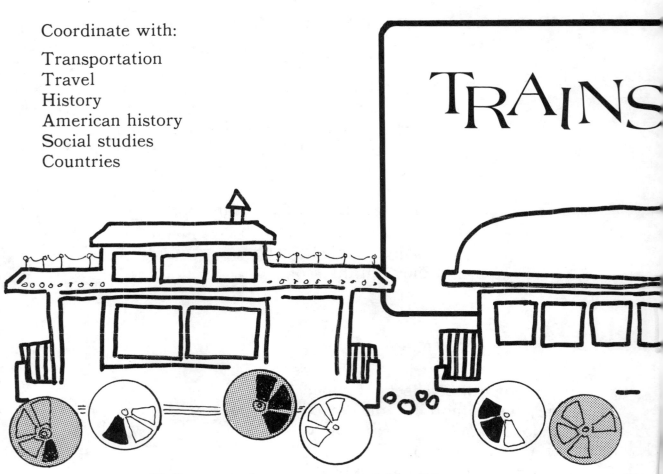

TRAINS

Tell your class to get comfortable. Relax. Close your eyes. We are going on a journey in our imagination. Listen and try to see the story unfold on the movie screen of your imagination . . . .

The sun is just going down. It sits over the horizon like a hesitant monarch, reluctant to leave its kingdom for the coming night. The heat of the long summer day hangs thick in the air and only the sound of birds can be heard . . . . You are sitting alongside the railroad track on the edge of town. The weeds are yellow and burned . . . dust seems to cover everything . . . . You are waiting for the next freight train . . . you are a bum . . . . Some people call you a drifter, a ne'er-do-well or a hobo. You have been living the life of the rail for many years now, and all of your worldly possessions are in one small cardboard suitcase tied with an old rope that sits next to you in the dust . . . . You have nowhere special to be going but you just think it is time to be moving on . . . . Fall will be in the air soon and winters aren't so hard to bear in the

TRAINS oo TRAINS

South . . . . So you sit and wait for the next southbound freight . . . patiently . . . quietly . . . and without fussing . . . . You know it may be an hour from now or it might be a day . . . . You sit for what seems like hours . . . . The sun is long gone and a large silvery moon is rising from the blackness of the horizon . . . . Suddenly you hear it . . . . A long low whistle . . . almost a moan . . . slides across the sky . . . . Again you hear it against the silent night . . . . And now you feel the vibrations of the train on the tracks . . . . It is coming . . . coming . . . coming . . . . You get up off the rock where you have been sitting . . . . Your small fire has about gone out, and you slowly kick dirt over it until it is only smoke and smolder . . . . The fields of wheat wave in the darkness around you, and way down the track you see the lights of a lonely farmhouse blink on . . . . The horizon is blood red and losing its color to fade to black . . . silhouettes of a line of telephone poles march across the flat land against the sky . . . . Looking up you see the first stars winking at the zenith as the shadows gather softly, thickly, and wrap around you, leaving you in a dark and sleeping countryside.

You climb the mounded rail bed, up through brambles and weeds . . . slipping . . . sliding . . . on the loose rocky incline . . . . You almost lose your balance, catch yourself on one hand then quickly jump up to the tracks . . . . You pull your worn and frayed coat more closely about you, wishing it still had a button or two; but they have been long gone . . . . There is a chill slowly spreading over the land and creeping up your sleeves . . . down your collar . . . . You shiver and pull the coat still closer about you . . . .

The whistle of the train floats forlornly across the now inky sky, and you know it has slowed to pass through town . . . . It will be moving very slowly when it reaches where you are waiting. With any luck an empty freight car will have an open door . . . . If not, there will always be another train . . . . Your fingers feel the chill now and your hands are feeling stiff, the cold nips your nose and both it and your eyes begin to run . . . . You wipe your eyes on your sleeve . . . . The train is very close now . . . . You feel it through your feet . . . . The engine strains, pulls . . . and struggles . . . to regain its speed . . . . Now you see the engine light flashing through the dark, and the tracks reflect the light like iron ribbons in the dark . . . . Just minutes and it will be here . . . . The ground rumbles, quivers, shakes . . . . The rails sing an almost inaudible, high-pitched whine as the train bears down . . . lumbering, straining . . . ponderously stretching into the night . . . . You step back as the mammoth engine thunders by and even your teeth rattle with its power . . . . Railroad cars slide by: clickety-clackety, clickety-clackety, clickety-clackety . . . there! . . . look! . . . an open door . . .! You run with the train . . . stumbling in the dark . . . almost falling . . . . You toss your case . . . thump . . . into the open car . . . now . . . reach out with both hands and grab at the edge of the door . . . . The train is gathering speed . . . . You feel it pulling at your arms . . . your shoulders . . . . You struggle to hold on and you . . . jump . . . propelling yourself up . . . into . . . the car . . . sprawled, spread-eagle on the floor . . . . You gasp for breath . . . . You made it . . . . You are heading South for the winter . . . . Open your eyes . . . . When you are ready, sit up.

Get your students into trios. Each group is going to plan a trip South for the winter. First brainstorm all the resources they may need: maps, weather information, almanacs, travel brochures, airline, train or bus information and prices, hotels, motels, cabins, etc. Several things will be part of this project:

1. Plan the trip by air and by land and compare prices and time. Also, don't forget costs of meals, gasoline, and motels along the way if you are driving.
2. Plan a wardrobe for a week. After it is complete, have students bring all the articles to class. Pile them on a table. Also bring **one** suitcase. Divide into groups of five. Each group is to rank order all the clothes and decide which articles are to be left behind. See if any of the groups can reach a consensus.
3. Get a driver's license booklet and see how much of the sample driver's test you can pass. Make large reproductions of the various kinds of traffic signs and hang them around the room. After a week, turn them to the wall and see how many students can identify them.

4. If you decide to go by air, list all the people who do jobs that make it possible for you to travel that way. Some examples are:

> ticket agents
> travel agents
> baggage handlers
> airplane mechanics
> air traffic controllers
> pilots
> flight attendants
> food service directors

88

Get into trios and have each trio select one of the professions listed above. They are to create an interview of ten of the most important questions they can think of to ask that person about his job and how it relates to travelers.

(89)

Make a collection of suitcases. Have each student bring some kind of suitcase or travel bag from home. Be sure you have hanging bags, shoulder bags, two-suiters, backpacks, etc. Pile and stack them in one corner. Over one night, place **one or two** objects in each bag. The next day get your students into trios and give each group one of the bags. Their first task is to decide what the person might look like who would carry that bag. Using large brown butcher paper, invite them to paint that character . . . life size. Then have them open the bag and see if they get any clues from the object inside about:

1. where the person is going
2. what the person looks like
3. what the person does for a living
4. how long he might be traveling

When all the traveling figures have been painted and all the decisions about who they are and where they are going have been made, tape them in a group on the wall in the hall and put their suitcases on the floor in front of them. Next to them on the wall put a one-page biography or autobiography (this is an excellent way to introduce biography and autobiography) which was created by the trio who created the character. Try being creative and overlap and group the characters as if they were a crowd in an airport.

(90)

Collect as many kinds of engines as you can, both models and pictures. Find out as many famous trains and names of trains as you can. For example, the **City of New Orleans** ran from Chicago to New Orleans. The **California Zephyr** ran from Chicago to San Francisco. Does anyone know where the **Orient Express** runs? Once you have found six or seven famous trains, break into groups and learn all about your train. Each group will make a presentation to the class . . . 10 minutes (no more) about their train that must include:

art
music
movement
images
pantomime

Using a large piece of cardboard, make a mock-up of the back end of a train. Ask your class if they know what a "whistle-stop" is and where the term came from. Talk about politicians and how they used to campaign from the back end of trains. Have each student become a historical candidate for President and **write a three-minute** campaign speech to be given from the back of the train. Present the speeches and videotape them. Let the class be the crowd. Be sure the end of your train looks as authentic as possible. Some vocabulary you may want to look for:

bunting	pullman	trestle
platform	diner	caboose
plank	whistle-stop	

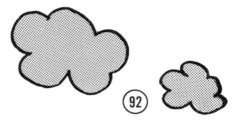

92

Find all the phrases you can that came from railroads.

What does it mean to be
"railroaded"?
"run out of town on a rail"?
"on the right track"?

93

Ask your students to bring model trains to class. Set one up and get it going. If you can collect enough track, get it to go all the way around the room.

When your students have brought many kinds of train cars to class, put them (students) into groups of five. Give each group a train car. Have them observe it closely and name as many parts as they can. Have them find three parts they **cannot** name and research what they find out. Then, as a class, draw a large, black-line drawing of a train engine, pullman, and caboose and label as many of the parts as you can.

94

Get your students into groups of six or eight. Student number one begins a story by saying, "I went to the train station and got out of the cab." The second student must say, "I went to the train station and I . . ." and then **act out the action without talking**. The third student must say, "I went to the train station and (act out action), and then I picked up my bags." The next student must say, "I went to the train station and (act out action); then I (act out action), and then I bought my ticket." The next student repeats all three actions (always nonverbally) and adds a new action. See how many actions can be remembered.

95

Make a collection of train music. There have been many songs written about trains:

"The Gambler"
"Chattanooga Choochoo"
"City of New Orleans"

just ducky

Coordinate with:

Birds
Migration
Climate
Weather
Social studies

(96) We are going on a trip in our imaginations. Get very comfortable. Lie down on the floor on your back. Close your eyes and breathe deeply for a minute or two while you think about your breath . . . . Ready . . . here we go . . . try to visualize this as clearly as you can . . . . You are standing in the shallow water at the edge of a lake in a high mountain valley. The water is cold . . . crystal . . . and clear. You stand perfectly still . . . watching the water carefully. You might be carved of white marble, you stand so still . . . . Suddenly your head darts beneath the water as you catch a small fish for breakfast . . . . You are what humans call a snow goose . . . and you have been living on this lake for the last three summer months. But the flock is getting restless now . . . honking . . . flying back and forth in short arcs . . . away from and back to the lake . . . . Something is about to happen. What is it, you wonder . . . you don't know . . . . You were born on this lake three months ago . . . pecking your way out of a large egg tucked into a nest of sticks in a hedgerow near the lake . . . . Now you look up at the sky . . . . It is bright blue against the sharp green of pines and sunny yellow of birches getting ready for winter . . . . All the birds around you are restless . . . stirring . . . rustling . . . waiting.

They seem to be getting ready for something . . . . Winter is coming to Canada . . . . You can feel it, too . . . . You look to the south and feel something urging you . . . pushing you to leap into the sky and head there . . . a longing to fly free . . . . The need grows stronger . . . but still you wait . . . . Perhaps today is the day . . . . Suddenly there is a flutter of wings . . . . All around you other geese are beginning to honk, honk, honk . . . as if to say, "It's time, it's time . . . ." A beating and rustle of wings . . . a few suddenly burst into the air . . . another and another . . . . Suddenly you are caught up with the feeling, stretch your wings . . . flap, flap, flap . . . and leap into the sky . . . . The sky is suddenly filled with white wings, beating the air . . . honking into the distance . . . filling the valley with a whirr . . . . You circle higher . . . yet higher . . . falling into a formation that somehow just seems right to you . . . . The flock honks . . . long lonely calls against the mountains, into the valleys, dips away from the clear mountain lake and heads . . . surely . . . purposely . . . and determinedly toward the south . . . . You knew it . . . it feels so right . . . you are on your way south for the winter . . . . Your wings will take you to a new land . . . a warmer climate . . . you honk . . . soar . . . and never look back . . . . Open your eyes . . . . When you are ready, sit up.

(97) Draw three columns on the chalkboard and label them. Under each column ask your students to brainstorm everything they know, or think they know, about each . . . and any information they can think of about any of them. Some examples to get started:

DUCKS	GEESE	SWANS
webbed feet	mean	long necks
mallard	nursery rhyme	black/white
ugly duckling	golden egg	fairy tale
waddle	Canadian	

Have students get into groups of three and decide which of the three they want to find out about. For each one they are to discover information in each area of the following web. When this is done, as a class compare and contrast all the similarities and differences you can find.

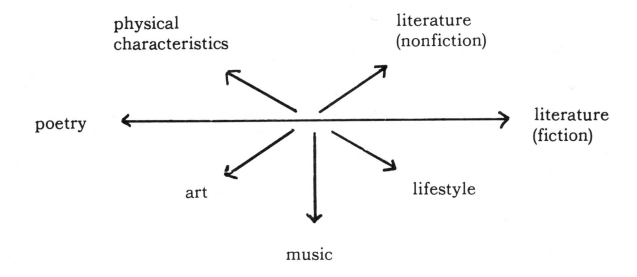

physical characteristics

literature (nonfiction)

poetry

literature (fiction)

art

lifestyle

music

Coordinate with:

Insects
Butterflies
Caterpillars
Conservation

don't BUG me

⁹⁸ Close your eyes. Get very comfortable. Relax. Breathe deeply and slowly. We are going on a trip in our imaginations . . . . You are in a very dark place. It is comfortable and cozy. You are curled up in a tight ball and you are very still . . . . You have been this way for most of the winter . . . resting, dreaming, sleeping and changing . . . changing . . . changing . . . . It is getting warmer as the days grow longer and spring begins to return to the earth . . . . You are beginning to feel tight and cramped and wish you could move . . . . You begin to wiggle and struggle . . . pushing, wriggling and trying to get out of the tiny pocket in which you find yourself . . . . You now have an overwhelming desire to get out of this small dark place . . . . You kick, squirm and claw at your tiny prison . . . stretching this way and that . . . . Now you see a small ray of light as you poke a hole through the wall of your tiny encasement . . . . It is tearing open . . . the sun is coming through . . . . Suddenly in a burst of light and air you are free . . . an explosion of light . . . a burst of cool wind, and a rush of crisp, intoxicating smells . . . . As your senses come alive, you realize you are damp and soggy . . . and the warmth of the sun is beginning to dry you . . . . Your wings . . . yes, your wings, are wrapped tightly

around you . . . . You push and stretch and begin to unfold them into the bright sunshine . . . slowly . . . slowly . . . slowly . . . they open and spread out into the air . . . . Warmth begins to flow into your legs, your body . . . and your wings . . . . They are drying now and opening into brilliant wings of vibrant purple, orange and lavender . . . black and yellow . . . specks of gold . . . . You feel a wonderful exhilaration . . . . You brush your wings gently back and forth in the air and feel the breeze rush around them . . . . It tries to lift you from your perch on a tiny twig . . . . Suddenly you are overwhelmed with the urge to fly . . . . You take a deep breath, and leap into the air on your brand-new wings . . . . You are a butterfly . . . . Relax . . . . Open your eyes . . . . When you are ready, you can sit up.

Get into partners. One partner has a large sheet of paper and lots of paints. Partner number one describes the butterfly he visualized while partner number two paints a picture of it to partner number one's satisfaction. Then reverse the experience.

Get into partners. One at a time each partner moves in the manner of a particular insect and adds a sound. The other partner tries to figure out what insect is being mimed. In five minutes see how many different insects can be identified.

Put your students into groups of 6 to 10. The first one reacts as if a bee had just stung him. The second one repeats that action and repeats a new one that relates to some kind of a bug. The third must repeat the first two actions and add a third . . . and so on until you get all around the circle. Brainstorm some of these possibilities to give students some ideas: . . . you found a roach in your cereal . . . you just swallowed a fly . . . you sat on a wasp . . . you found a tick on your neck . . . you were bitten by a mosquito . . . you felt a gnat in your eye . . . .

Kids love this. Each pair of students is to go to an encyclopedia and find a picture of a "bug." First brainstorm all the categories you might try:

spiders	butterflies
insects	worms
caterpillars	beetles
moths	ants
flies	what else?

When they have found a picture of a bug they particularly like, give them a **large** piece of paper, the bigger the better. They are to draw and paint in full color, their bug . . . as big as they can . . . and as lifelike as they can. When everyone is finished, cut them out and make a giant "bug" collage on one wall or over the windows.

Partners sit opposite each other. Discuss obstacles insects encounter and how they get around them. One partner is blindfolded. The second builds a maze on the tabletop from assorted objects. Then the blindfolded partner "walks" two fingers through the maze using only the directions given by his partner. When this is done, reverse the process with a new maze.

Get into partners. Partner one is a fish in a pesticide-laden stream. He tries to convince partner one . . . now a farmer . . . not to use pesticides. After one minute, reverse roles and go for another minute. Do the same with each of the following:

an ant trying to convince a child not to step on it

a fly trying to convince a mean young child not to pull off its wings

a mosquito trying to convince a frog not to eat it

a butterfly trying to convince a caterpillar that it is beautiful

a worm convincing a fish not to eat it

a spider being convinced by a gnat not to wrap it up in its web

a silkworm trying to get the farmer not to steal its silk for cloth

In each of the above situations, encourage the students to come up with as many arguments and points of view as they can think of. Then share the different reasoning and ideas with the entire class in a group discussion.

You will need several students to collect enough grasshoppers so everyone in the class will have one in a bottle. Have each student draw the grasshopper as carefully as he can from direct observation . . . while it is hopping around in the bottle.

(105)

Following the activity on the preceding page, have the students diagram what they imagine a grasshopper's internal organs and digestive system are like. After this is done . . . research this topic and find an authentic representation of the inside of a grasshoper. First compare this to your students' drawings. Were they close? Then compare it to a human being's digestive system and internal organs. How are they different? How are they the same?

 (106)

For this activity you will need newspaper, pipe cleaners, drinking straws, crayons, construction paper, tape and glue. Allow the students to form groups of five. There will be one living insect for each team . . . all different. However, the insect will be placed in another room and one group member will serve as the runner between the insect and the rest of the group.

Each group is to use any of the available materials to make a giant model of the insect that will be described to them by their runner. The runner may **not** touch any materials and can only describe. The runner may make as many trips to look at the insect as is necessary. The runner may use any word or words to describe the insect but must keep his hands behind his back at all times. The groups will have 15 minutes to create their insects.

 (107)

Using resource materials and tagboard, students will make sports cards from the tagboard, using baseball cards as models but with insects as the players. The front should have a picture of the insect with the sport it plays. Be sure the sport is appropriate for the insect. The back should have the vital statistics for that insect. The cards can later be traded, categorized in many different ways . . . or . . . in groups of three have students create a new game that can be played with the insect sports cards.

(108)

Brainstorm insect sounds. Prepare the students to be part of an orchestra of insect sounds. In partners they are to decide on a sound and create it either vocally or synthetically. Choose a rhythmic count. Combine the sounds, the rhythm and anything else needed to create an insect symphony. Tape the results . . . then discuss how it can be improved . . . . Revise it and tape it again . . . .

NOODLING AROUND

OODLES OF NOODLES

Gotta make spaghetti
Threw it in a pot.
Grabbed a bag of noodles,
You know a little makes a lot.

Stirred it up, boiled it down
Watched the noodles bubble,
As they boiled, as they cooked,
They doubled and redoubled!

They grew and swelled and overflowed
Getting bigger as they cooked.
The package had instructions,
I guess I should have looked.

So I fed my baby sister some.
Ate a plate myself.
Froze some for November and
Stuffed some on the shelf.

Sent a baggy full to Grandma
and a pound to Uncle Jack.
And still I had enough to fill
Another grocery sack.

Poodles won't eat noodles,
I should know, I tried.
Goldfish won't eat noodles,
I tried it and they died.

These noodles first were ankle deep,
Then they reached up to my knees.
Now I'm in noodles to my nose,
Won't someone help me, please?

They spilled out, down the stairs,
And slithered under doors,
Across the porch and down the walk,
Now they've filled the empty lot.

Soon I fear the house will be
Submerged in noodles going wild.
The house, the car, and Fred the cat.
What have you done my child?

So remember when you fix 'em
When you throw them in a pot,
Read directions carefully,
Cuz a little makes a LOT.

Read the poem on the preceding page to your class. Let them hear it two or three times; then divide them into partners or trios for each verse and let them create movements for their verse. (These should be movements that can be done **in their seats**.) Then each group will teach the entire class their movements for their verse. Finally, read the poem and have everyone do all the movements as you share the poem.

Present it to other classes.
Present it to the PTO.

Use the poem to brainstorm all the things your class can think of that sometimes goes wrong.

(110)

Bring one package of noodles to class, a hot plate, and a large pan. Have each student estimate what volume the noodles will be when they are cooked. Then cook them and measure. The trick is to have each pair of partners make their estimation in a different kind of measurement. Have one pair estimate the number of cups. Another must think in pints, another in quarts. Have others estimate in liters, gallons, ounces and/or pounds. After you have them cooked and drained, the task is to find out how much you have by volume and by weight and **convert** that to the appropriate measure.

(111)

Put your students into partners and give them the following instructions: **one** at a time each of you do something, nonverbally, that goes wrong at times. See if your partner can tell you what you are doing . . . then describe a time when the same thing happened to him.

(112)

The problem in the poem resulted from not having read the instructions for making the noodles. Get your students into trios and have them make a list of all the things they can think of that require following directions.

(113)

Divide your class into groups of six. Each group is given an object . . . treasure to hide. They are to hide it somewhere in or around the school. Then they are to make a "treasure" map that will lead another team to the treasure. The only rule is that each direction on the map must be a riddle. In order to get students aware of riddles, bring some riddle books from the library and share them for two or three days before you do this activity. Then the groups trade "maps" and find their treasures by solving the riddles and following the clues the maps give.

(115)

(114)

Place a table in front of the room with a pile of assorted objects on one end. Tell your students that they must each write a set of directions for carefully arranging all the objects artfully on the other end of the table. Their directions should be step by step and give the reader the exact procedure for moving the objects and arranging them. After they have done this, ask for a volunteer. The volunteer comes up to the table. One student reads the **entire** set of directions while the volunteer listens. When this is done, the volunteer tries to arrange the items according to the directions he has heard and tried to remember. Begin with only three to four items and see if you can work your way up to ten.

On a table in front of the room, place a pair of large coveralls and a jacket. (Be dressed casually for this.) Tell your students that they are to write you a set of specific instructions for putting on the coveralls and the jacket. Give them the time to do this; then ask for a volunteer to read their instructions. As he does, you follow them **literally and exactly**. This almost always leads to laughter, comedy and miscommunication. If the reader says, "First put one foot in the coveralls," put one foot up on the table and stick it into the coveralls. Then the reader will go back and say, "First pick up the coveralls." You will reach out with both hands and pick them up in a ball and hold them out in front of you waiting for the next instructions. When it definitely is not working, have them go back to their writing and try to be more explicit. They will get better at it as they work. The point is to illustrate how important clear instructions are and also how important it is that they be interpreted correctly.

For this activity you will need a small budget. Buy six small model cars at a hobby shop, but buy two each of the **same** model. Divide your class into six groups. Give each group a model to build. Each two groups will have the same model. One of the groups is to read and follow the instructions **exactly.** Their counterparts with the same model will find that they have **no** instructions and must put theirs together by "guess and by golly." Give them a time limit . . . perhaps one class period and then compare the results.

Which groups got more done?

Which groups felt more frustration?

Which groups had to take things apart and start again?

Which groups had a better product at the end of the time?

Get your students into partners when they go to lunch. On the first lunch day, partner number one is to give number two the exact instructions for eating lunch. Number two cannot and must not do anything until he is given the instruction on how to do it. Number one gives one instruction and number two does it immediately. Number one gives a second instruction and number two then follows it as carefully as possible. They continue until lunch has been eaten. On the second day reverse the process.

Discuss:

1. Did you feel frustration at not being able to go on until you were told to do so?
2. Did you get your lunch eaten?
3. Would you rather have one instruction at a time or several?
4. How many could you follow at one time without forgetting?

me and my shadow

Coordinate with:

Science
Solar system
Color
Photography ⑱

You need a sunny day.
Take your class out onto the blacktop or the playground where shadows can be observed. Invite your students to:
- make the longest shadow they can
- make the widest, shortest, etc.
- see if they can make a shadow that is continuous even though they don't touch each other
- notice what happens when the shadows of two objects overlap. Is it darker? Is there any division? Can you tell the difference?

At noon when the shadows are very short, go out with a large sheet of paper and a marker. Stand with your short, squat shadow on the paper and draw around it. Then, as a homework assignment, have your students go home with a marker and a large sheet of paper and wait until five or six in the evening and have them do the same thing when shadows are long and narrow. Cut out the two shadows and hang them on the wall together. Compare them. On each of them write words that describe them and compare the words: long, short, fat, narrow, etc.

(119)

(120)

(121)

Make a collection of objects in a box. Set up an overhead and mask it so no one can see what is sitting on it. Place the objects on the overhead in unusual positions and see if your students can identify the objects. Then **overlap** two or three objects on the overhead at the same time and see if they can still identify them. You may choose to use objects that relate to an area of study, a content area or a story you are reading.

Have each student do this at home: Make an **unusual** shadow, cut it out, paste it on a contrasting background. When they all come to class, hang these all over the room and number them. Have your students make a list and write down all the things they think each one could be. Encourage them to come up with as many possibilities as they can. Then, each day, let one or two students reveal what their objects are.

Get your students into partners. Have them sit side by side at a table with scissors, paper and glue. Partner #1 is to do something in slow motion. (Cut out a word or shape and glue it to a contrasting background.) Partner #2 is to try to be #1's perfect shadow, doing exactly the same thing as number one works. This encourages observation and patterning skills. The goal is for both of them to be working as closely together as possible.

A silhouette is an object in shadow against a strong backlight. Hang a sheet in your classroom with an overhead focused on it from the back. Have ten students go behind the sheet and "mill" around. When you give a signal, all but one of them is to leave the light. (They must decide who this is to be.) That person will "pose" and hold perfectly still. The rest of the classroom is to try to identify this student from the silhouette. Make sure everyone has a chance.

Follow up the above activity by having each student think of a way to "disguise" his silhouette. Discuss how hats, clothing, pillows, etc., might change the silhouettes. Now repeat the above activity but with the "disguises."

Give each student a letter of the alphabet. Use both upper and lower cases. The student's task is to make a shadow that is in the form of his letter from the shadow of something else. The shadow must fit on an 11" x 14" sheet of paper. Replace your standard alphabet above your board with this new shadow alphabet.

Shadow collages can be made using photo paper and a photo enlarger. In a darkroom under a yellow safelight, take a sheet of photo paper. Arrange cutouts, fabric, lace, leaves, gauze, etc., on the paper. Turn on the enlarger for three seconds. Then drop the sheet into a tray of developer for one to two minutes and then into fixer. Then wash in clear water. The results can be absolutely magical. Discuss opaque, clear, and translucent materials. Let students experiment and see how many kinds of images can be made. Try things like, moving objects slowly while exposing the paper, adding things and taking things away during exposure, turning the light off and on while adding or removing objects. See what else your students can do. This can be done using objects from an area of study, from a story or poem, or as illustrations for a story they are writing.

(123)

Have students get into trios. One of them will be the sun, one the moon and the other the earth. Let them figure out how those three heavenly bodies move in relationship to each other and actually begin to move "around" each other. Then figure out the relative positions when we see the eclipse of the moon, then an eclipse of the sun. It is even more fun, then, to give the "sun" a flashlight, darken the room and shine its light toward the earth and moon. Can you figure out an eclipse?

"The Shadow of Your Smile" and invite your students to paint shadows of invite your students to paint shadows of love, anger, happiness, fear, etc. Label these **The Shadow of Your Fear**, etc. This is a good vehicle for discussing feelings.

You will need:
 An enlarger (You surely have at least one parent who is an amateur photographer.)
 Developer and Fixer (Complete instructions for mixing these is on the can . . . and it is **easy**.)
 Yellow safelight
These are all available at any photo store.

(125)

(126)

A variation of the last activity is to have each student make a **creature at home** . . . and to draw or paint its shadow. Then on Monday everyone brings his creature to class and displays it on one side of the room. On Tuesday everyone brings the shadow he made of his creature and hangs it on the opposite wall. You may have students bring them to you, mix them up and hang them so no one knows to whom they belong. Now, students get into pairs and each pair tries to match each creature with its proper shadow.

Arrange a stack of blocks, boxes and tubes and shine one strong light on it from above and at an angle. Your students are to draw it by shading in **only** the shadow areas. They can make **no lines**. The shadows should all be the same darkness . . . . Tell your students to let the shadows run together just as they do without trying to define the objects. See what happens to the image drawn in this way.

What color is a shadow? Can you make shadows of different colors? What actually causes the color you see in a shadow? Now, take three strong flashlights and a large sheet of white paper, or better still a sheet. Cover the ends of the flashlights with colored gelatin: red, yellow, and blue. Darken the room and shine the three lights on the sheet. Put something or someone in the lights and light them with the three colored lights from all kinds of angles. Can you make different colored shadows? Do the colors "mix"? Can you make one person or object have more than one shadow?

(127)

Have each student create an imaginary "creature." Then shine a light on it, make its shadow and paint its shadow on a white sheet of paper. The above is done secretly so his partner does **not** see the creature. Then partners swap **shadows** of their creatures. Their task now is to look at the shadow and to create the creature it belongs to . . . just by looking at the creature's shadow. Then compare creatures and see how similar or different they are.

MAGICAL THREES

(128)

Coordinate with:

Storytelling
Plot development
Paragraph development

This is an exciting way to get students into storytelling as well as utilizing person, place and action.

Divide your class into trios. Give each trio this assignment: Each one of them is to take an 8" x 10" tagboard card and glue a picture from a magazine on it. In each trio you must have red, blue and yellow tagboard. Everyone with red will find a picture of a **character**. Everyone with blue tagboard will find a picture of a **place**, and everyone with yellow tagboard must find a picture of a **problem** situation where something is happening. (Any characters in this last picture can be ignored or can be supporting characters.)

72

When the preceding is done, have each trio look at their three pictures and see if they can put them together, verbally into a story. After they have talked about it for a few minutes, say "Switch." Everyone in the class gets up, takes his card with him and finds two people with which to form a **new** trio . . . but the new trio must include a red, blue and yellow card (person, place, problem). These new trios look at their three pictures and try to put **them** together to make a new story. Keep switching and talking and switching and talking. This can be done many different times and with many different sets of pictures.

Try using the above activity with pictures taken from the content you are studying. If you are studying Japan, make the pictures the students find be Japanese. Get the idea?

Now tell your students you are going to make one last switch. They are to find two partners . . . . Sit down and not only talk about the story, but begin to write it down. Encourage them to try at least three different story possibilities before they decide on the one they want to use. When they have decided, write a rough draft. Then the next day, come back and do a rewrite . . . and finally do a finished story. Take all the stories from all the trios and put them into a book that anyone can read. Or put them on the wall. Or share them with each other . . . or illustrate them . . . or present them to the PTO . . . .

A nice variation for this activity is to give each student a "dot" sticker. These are available at an office supply. They should be in the three colors just as the previous activity: red, blue, yellow. This time when they break up to find two new partners, each has his sticker on his forehead! Now each can visually find his new partner by this colored dot.

(131)

Put a large box in the corner of your room. Invite students to bring interesting objects from home and put them into the box. Encourage them to think of things from the kitchen, garage, basement, attic, office or den, etc. When you have a wide range of items, begin the following activity:

Have three students come up and, without talking to each other, each takes **one object from the box**. Put the rest of the class into trios and their task will be to write a sentence . . . or a paragraph . . . or a story that includes the three objects. Do this once each day for a week.

The second week add the following restriction:

In your paragraph or story, one of the objects must be used in a way in which it was **not** intended.

The third week change the restriction to:

In your story, one of the objects must be magic.

Some restrictions you can use that will challenge students further and encourage creative thinking could be:

One of the objects must have dried blood on it.

One of the objects must be broken.

One of the objects must be three times its normal size.

Two of the objects must be very, very old.

One of the objects must be a fake.

One of the objects must carry a message.

One of the objects must have been found in an unusual place.

One of the objects was left at the door in the middle of the night.

One of the objects was a murder weapon.

A variation of the above is to put students into trios. Place three objects on the table in front of the room. They are tagged:

People's exhibit #1: Found at the bottom of the stairs.
People's exhibit #2: Found clutched in the victim's left hand.
People's exhibit #3: Found stuffed underneath a sofa cushion.

Each trio is to then create a mystery story using the three tagged objects as the significant "clues" to the identity of the murderer.

Send three students out into the neighborhood with a Polaroid camera. They are to take three photographs. When they bring them back into the class, display them in front. Put your class into trios. Their task is to write a mystery using the three photos as clues.

74

A ROSE IS A ROSE

Coordinate with:

Botany
Plant reproduction
Seeds, flowers
Career education

(133)   Close your eyes . . . . Get very comfortable . . . . We are going on a short journey in our imaginations . . . . See yourself getting smaller and smaller. You are no longer you; you are a hard, dry and very tiny seed. You are buried in the dark, rich soil, and you are frozen solid. It is the dead of winter and nothing about you stirs . . . . You are waiting . . . waiting . . . waiting . . . for what you know will eventually happen . . . . Slowly you become aware that it is getting slightly warmer around you, the earth is beginning to soften . . . it is still too cold to grow and most of the earth is still frozen, but the temperature is slowly rising. The ground is now growing warm, and you feel tiny trickles of water running by you in the soil. You are getting damp and a bit warmer . . . you feel the soil growing warmer and warmer . . . it is damp and you are getting soaked clear through . . . . You feel yourself stir deep down inside, and something in you urges you to push and stretch and find a way out of your shell . . . . You are beginning to grow . . . . You split your shell and push a tiny tendril out into the now warm soil . . . . You stretch and curl and reach toward the light . . . toward the sunshine . . . . At the same time you begin to send a tiny root down into the soil looking for water and other nutrients . . . . Your tiny shoot suddenly breaks through the soil and the light is so bright, so warm, so inviting that you suddenly

begin to grow faster . . . . The sun feels so good on your skin . . . . You uncurl two tiny leaves and bask in the warmth of the sun and grow even more quickly . . . . You are stretching up and up now . . . popping out leaves as you go . . . . At your top you form a tiny bud that day by day grows larger and larger . . . round, firm . . . bulging, pushing, and it suddenly **pops** open and your petals fold out, opening to the world . . . . You are a bright color; you are dizzy with the process of becoming . . . . You are in full blossom, smiling and shining at the garden around you. You see that the garden is full of other flowers . . . many colors . . . all shapes and sizes . . . . A bee buzzes by and hovers about your petals . . . . Landing carefully, it crawls down into you, gathering nectar and getting pollen all over its legs . . . . When it has drunk its fill, it quickly flies away to its hive . . . . You bask in the sun . . . . You are enjoying a soft spring rain shower that happens by to give you a long cool drink. Life is wonderful. You have been blossoming for over a week now, and you notice that there are tiny brown spots on the edges of your petals. Your head is getting weak and is beginning to droop . . . . Dozens of bees have visited you and carried away the nectar they will turn to honey . . . . Your petals are getting browner and browner . . . losing their color . . . . You are fading . . . slowly fading. Several of your petals have fallen off . . . the rest are now brown, crinkly and dry. A wind comes up and buffets you back and forth . . . . The rest of your petals are torn away and fly freely on the wind . . . . You are a stem . . . . You open the last of the heart of your bud and let loose your seeds . . . flinging them into the wind to perhaps land in a garden and grow at another time in another place . . . . You are very tired now and you lie down on the ground . . . . Your leaves are brown, coming apart . . . disintegrating and returning back to the soil . . . . You will make good mulch for next year's flowers. It is time for you to be quiet now, to rest . . . . When you are ready, open your eyes . . . sit up . . . .

You are going to do the same guided fantasy again, only this time explain to your class that as you do it, they are to actually move their bodies to the story as if they really were the seed becoming the plant and growing into a flower. First have them find a space where they will not run into anyone else as they grow. Have them get as small and still as they can and then begin the imagination exercise over again.

Following the above fantasy, you may have one flowering chrysanthemum plant in your room. This should have enough blossoms on it so that you can give every student one flower with a stem and some leaves. Explain the six main parts of almost every flower: stem, leaves, sepals, petals, stamen, anther. Have everyone find each of these parts on his blossom.

(136)

Invite a flower arranger to class to actually create an arrangement in front of the class. Ask him to explain what and why they do what they do and to explain a bit about color, balance, visual interest, etc.

(137)
First collect ten small vases and arrange them in a row on a small table at the front of your room. Make friends with a local florist. Explain what you are doing and get him to donate one each of ten different flowers. Put one in each of the vases at the front of your room.

(138)
Get into partners. Have each partner pick the flower he thinks is the most beautiful. Give each one minute to convince his partner to his point of view. Then when this is done talk about point of view, personal taste . . . and hopefully let them decide that there is really no "right" or "wrong" answer here.

(139)
Place the flowers around the room and let students pick one that they are going to sit down by and draw as carefully and in as much detail as possible. Encourage them to observe the tiniest of details and to include them in their drawings. Do this with soft artists' drawing pencils.

(140) Divide into trios and move about observing the flowers. In each case have the trios try to identify the six main parts of each flower. Some will fool you. Example: bougainvillea petals are really not petals; it is actually the leaves that turn color, as does the poinsettia. What we think of as the petals are actually the leaves .... The flower itself is really very tiny.

In trios, brainstorm and make a list of all the events where flowers are very important or play a major role, for example, weddings, graduations, etc.

(141) Compare Oriental flower arranging and its philosophy with Occidental ideas about flower arranging. Try to create some Oriental arrangements with your class.

(142)

Go to a large nursery. Buy a pack of flower seeds. Marigolds are good for this. Explain what you are doing and get the florist to donate enough tiny pots and some soil for your classroom. Everyone can then plant his own seed and raise a flower. Draw it at different stages. Identify its parts ... when it has dried and lets loose its seeds. Keep the seeds in a dry place for several months and then try planting them .... See if you can observe the "cycle" over again.

(143)

Divide your class into trios. Give each trio one of the following gardens to research. When they have done so, they must present their findings to the class and must have used:
1. something visual
2. at least one poem or song
3. something using movement, role playing or acting out

Formal Garden   Elizabethan
Rose Garden   Herb Garden
Topiary Garden   Rock Garden
Japanese Tea Garden Victory Garden
Emerald Garden   Sunken Garden
Covent Garden

(144)

Draw a flower in four panels in each of four different stages: young stem with bud, blossoming, wilted, dying or dead. Discuss the following question: Is one stage any more beautiful than another? Why? Why not? Are there any right or wrong answers to this question? Then take a look at the book **Flowers** by Irving Penn. He is a famous photographer of flowers and has photographed them in all of their stages of living and dying. See if you can find beauty in all of the stages.

(145)

Make a large map of the United States. Find out the state flower for each state and fill in the state with paintings of that flower. You will end up with a beautiful United States in full "blossoming" color.

Coordinate with:

History
Inventions
Cultures
Geography
Self-concept

(146)

The motivation for these activities is wonderful . . . students enjoy it and it is good for self-concept development. Ask each student to bring something from home that he plays with or **used** to play with that is very old and to also bring something that is very new . . . within the last year or two. Make a collection of these "toys" around the edges of your classroom.

Place all the toys that move by themselves in front of the room and turn them on at the same time . . . **watch them go!** While you are doing this have students, in partners, write down all the words they can think of that would describe the way the different toys are moving. Encourage them to think of as many words as they can for as many different toys as they can. Be sure they have at least one word for every toy.

Now, each student finds a new partner. One at a time he shares a description and sees if his partner can pick out the specific toy that was being described. (147)

Push back the chairs. Everyone gets up and finds a place in the open space. When you begin the music, each student is to pick a particular toy that is sitting somewhere in the classroom and begin to move as that toy. When the music stops, each quickly gets a partner, moves as his chosen toy and sees if his partner can tell which toy he is mimicking. (148)

Have each student pick a toy and put it into a paper bag. Give him three minutes to look at it very closely, and very carefully, noting as much detail as possible. Now, he is to describe it to a partner. The partner may ask as many questions as he likes. When they are finished, the second person is to describe the toy to a third and the third is to draw a picture of it. Again, as many questions as are necessary may be asked. Then have the three compare the original toy with the drawing that resulted from the activity. Are they alike? How are they different?

Where did the communication break down?

Where was the communication very clear and concise?

What specific words can you think of that were misinterpreted?

How would you do this differently if you were to do it again?

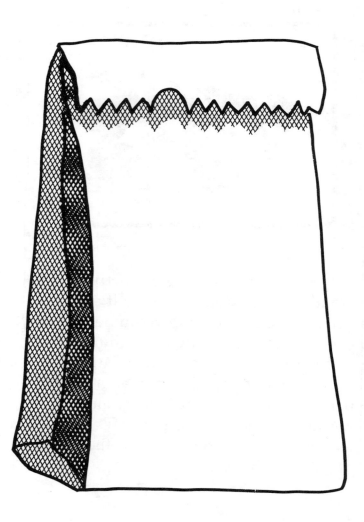

Get into partners and have each student bring an old toy with him. Give him ten minutes to describe it to his partner:

1. Where did he get that toy?
2. Why is it important to him?
3. What event does the toy particularly remind him of?

(149)

Put students into groups of three. Put one toy in the middle of their group. They are to take fifteen minutes to "redesign" that toy to make it:

1. more asthetically pleasing
2. more durable
3. more fun
4. useful as well as fun
5. fun for a specific age group:
   5-year-old
   10-year-old
   25-year-old

(152)

Get students into trios, each with a toy. When you say "Begin," number 1 will begin to talk about his toy. When you say "Switch," number 2 will talk, and then number 3. But each time give them categories to talk about in relation to the toy and change the category each time: For example:

Talk about its **color**.
Now talk about its **size**.
Now talk about its **shape**.
Now talk about its **material**.

Some of the other categories that can be discussed could include:

texture
uses
durability
unusual characteristics
changes you would like to make it better

(150)

Give your students, in groups of three, three toys. They are to create a new toy using ideas or parts from each of the three toys in front of them. When they have done this, have them draw first a blueprint or diagram of their new toy . . . and then a full-color rendering of it and present it to the class. Be sure they can explain how they got ideas from the original toys and how they applied to the new one.

Divide your class into groups of five. Have each group select a country of the world and then research some of the toys that have come out of that country. As a group organize a presentation for the class that will communicate the information you have discovered. However, each presentation must:

1. use music
2. have at least one visual element
3. require listeners to participate at least once.

Get your students into groups of eight—exactly. In each group there will be four sets of partners. Have them stand in a circle with partner opposite. When you say "Begin," have them describe a toy to their partners. This means that four people are talking at the same time. As they talk, have them slowly back up. The task in each pair is to focus on the partner and try to exclude what he is hearing from the other three teams. When they are finished, about 3 minutes, partner number two will tell back to number one what he heard him say. Then repeat the experience with the other partner going first.

Have students bring to school the box a toy came in. In small groups have them first brainstorm questions they would like to ask the manufacturer. Then have them write the letter and send it off to the maker of the toy. When and **if** an answer comes, staple it to the bulletin board with the box the toy came in.

Some sample questions students might want to ask:

1. Is this toy safe for a 2-year-old?
2. Is the paint lead free?
3. What groups of youngsters "tested" this toy?
4. How is the cost of a toy determined?
5. How long does the average toy stay on the market?

First write the following words on your chalkboard in large block letters:

Larger
Smaller
Add something
Remove something
Change color
Change material
Combine
Rearrange
Add sound

Now get your students into groups of five or six. In the center of each group, place one of the toys. Their task is to **improve** the toy by using any of the above ideas in any combinations. They are to take all the stops out and generate as many different ideas as they can. When they are finished, have them pick at least three new versions of their toy to share with the class and tell why they think it would be better.

Get into groups of five. Each group will play the following games for one minute at a time using **only** their imagination, no real equipment:

Jacks	Spin the Bottle	Four Square
Marbles	Sorry	Tic-tac-toe
Tiddly-winks	Old Maid	Cat's Cradle

After they are finished, give them time to talk about what happened and how successful they were at communicating ideas with their bodies.

Get your students into partners of one girl and one boy. Have them bring their toys with them. As a team have them list all the characteristics of each toy. How are they the same? How are they different? Do they reflect different roles or expectations? Are boys' toys more or less violent or physically aggressive than the girls' toys? Do they like this difference? Is it fair? What is it telling them? Do they agree?

After students have created a new toy, they are to create an advertising campaign for it. They will do three things:

Design a billboard for the toy.

Write a jingle and TV commercial for it.

Create a magazine ad for your toy.

Coordinate with:

Careers
U.S. history
Social studies
Self-concept

bridges

First, some preparation will be in order. In each of six stacks, place one Sunday edition of a newspaper, two rolls of masking tape and a brick. Divide your class into six groups around the stacks on the floor and give them the following directions:

You have fifteen minutes. You need to build the longest, highest bridge you can build with these materials. Your bridge will be tested by dropping several objects on it from one foot high in the following sequence:

tennis ball
baseball
basketball
brick

The object is to build the strongest bridge you can from the materials presented.

After the above has been done and the bridges tested, each group should discuss how they might make their bridge stronger. Several days later, repeat the exercise and see if the decisions the groups made actually result in stronger bridges.

Invite your students to get on the floor and find their "own space." When you say "Begin," they are to alternately show their partner ways to make bridges with parts of their bodies. In three mintues they are to make as many bridges with their bodies as they can, in as many different ways as they can.

Get your students into partners and have them brainstorm all the bridges they can think of that are not bridges. For example:

hugs
smiles
letters
notes
winks

Now get your student into trios. They are to now make bridges in different ways by putting all three students together into one bridge. After this has been done, they can then get into groups of four or five and make "multiple person" bridges.

When they have reached this point, have them try each of the following specific bridges:

> covered bridge
> pontoon bridge
> suspension bridge
> stone bridge
> drawbridge
> swinging bridge
> foot bridge
> a one-log bridge

Have students collect as many pictures of bridges as they can and organize them in different ways: by culture, historically, by material, length, height. Any other ways they can think of?

In trios have students discuss how the following are and are not like bridges:

kiss	phonograph record
conversation	radio
cold shoulder	argument
telephone line	pouting
sewer pipe	anger
airplane	party
lighthouse	school bus

Run off copies of "Bridge over Troubled Water" by Simon and Garfunkel. Then play it in your classroom. So many questions can be dealt with in this song.

What is friendship?

How far will you go with a friend?

Is friendship as much a commitment as marriage?

(165) Sit together with your partner and compare **one** sentence, the simplest sentence you can write that would accurately define the essence of the word **bridge**. After you have done that, have several of them shared in the classroom. Then go to the dictionary and find out what it has to say about it. Then have your students, in partners, discuss with each other each of the following:

How is a rainbow like a bridge?

How is a train like a bridge?

Think of several bridges that cannot be seen.

Name as many famous bridges as you can.

What does it mean to "burn all your bridges"?

If you could build a magical bridge to somewhere, where would it be?

If you could build a bridge into your imagination, what would it look like? Show each other with paint or pastels.

What is meant by an "unabridged" dictionary?

(166) Trolls, we are told, live under bridges. Read "Three Billy Goats Gruff" to your class. What is the moral of this story? What do you think the troll looked like? Was he in the right? Who had the right-of-way? How might the goats have gotten across the bridge safely? What does this story mean?

(167) Everyone find a space. When I say "Begin," you are to begin climbing across the bridge I tell you is there before you. As you cross this bridge, I will magically change it into different kinds of bridges. See if your body can **show** the kind of bridge you are crossing. Begin to cross a rope bridge . . . now it just changed into a swinging bridge . . . a board across a stream . . . a log over a chasm . . . a slippery ice bridge . . . it is beginning to melt . . . a hanging ladder bridge . . . .

(168) Get your students into trios and tell them their task as a group is to take something **real** and change it into **fantasy** by using one of the following bridges:
paint, words, pictures, music, poetry, dance, drama.

Did you know that the famous London Bridge was taken apart one piece at a time and reassembled in Arizona? It is now a tourist attraction.

Put your students into groups of 5 or 6 with a set of Lego's. Their task is first to build an interesting bridge. Then they are to write a step-by-step set of instructions for building that bridge . . . or an exact replica of it. Then all groups tear down their bridges and exchange sets of directions. From their new set of directions they are to try to duplicate the bridge described. When everyone is finished, be sure they have time to discuss why communication may have been misinterpreted, where it was incomplete and where it was very clear.

This is all about signs and symbols. We use them every day. First run off a copy of the next page. This is just one area where we use signs and symbols. How many of your students can explain the meanings of all of these signs?

(169)

Get your students into partners and have them first interpret the meanings of these signs. Then have them create a new set of signs to communicate the same messages but in a different and perhaps better way. When this is done, have them exchange their new signs several times around the classroom and see how many of their classmates can interpret the new signs correctly.

What makes a sign readable?
What makes it communicate easily?
Why do we all interpret a good sign the same way?

walk, don't run

Coordinate with:

Cities
Communication
Self-concept
Social studies

NO
PASSING
ZONE

R R

(170)

Get your students into partners. Each is to design a billboard advertising himself as the world's best friend. After students have discussed size, color, visability, etc., they are to actually make the billboard.

(171)

In partners create a bumper sticker . . . . Get some plain yellow Con-Tact paper, cut it into strips and let the students actually make real, stick-on bumper stickers. These can be put on their family cars (with permission) . . . or call them locker stickers and start a new trend. Con-Tact peals off cleanly if removed within six to eight weeks.

(172)

How many **universal** signs can you think of that we all recognize? Make a collection of these: Red Cross, Coca-Cola, R.R. crossing, stop, barber pole, car symbols like Chevrolet, VW for Volkswagen and then what about designer clothes?

(173)

Sometimes we all need some quiet time. Students are to design **do not disturb** signs for themselves. They will make two of them, seal them between two layers of clear Con-Tact paper and have them for use at home and at school. When they really need some quiet time, they can stick them to their desks and for 15 minutes no one will bother them. This goes for the teacher as well, so make one for yourself. At home, have them discuss this idea with their parents. They and their parents must reach an agreement as to how long and how often this sign can be used.

Discuss with your classroom how or if this sign could become either an escape or a "cop out."

(174)

In partners come up with all the hand signs we use and generally understand. Some of these might be thumbs up, peace, O.K., thumbing a ride, saluting, waving, shaking hands, etc. Now each pair of partners is to create ten new hand signs for different things that only the two of them will know.

Go to the driver's license bureau and "borrow" or get a **Rules of the Road** book for every student. Have them learn all the signs shown in the book. How many other "signs" do we use to control traffic? Brainstorm all of these ideas. Some possibilities might be traffic lights, barricades, left turn signals, traffic officers with flashlights, traffic watch radio announcers, freeway exit signs, etc.

(176)

Go to a paper company and "borrow" several large sheets of cardboard (a box company is good for this, too). Get students into groups of three. Their task is to:

1. Brainstorm all the signs that might be useful to have up in the hall in the building somewhere.
2. Choose one they like the best or that they think is the most important of all their ideas.
3. Create a sign to communicate that idea.
4. Duplicate it on the large sheet of cardboard.
5. Hang it in the appropriate place in the building.

Be sure you encourage them to consider size, shape, color, impact, location, height (eye level? lower? higher?).

(177)

Consider all the other areas where we use signs. How many can your class brainstorm and list on the chalkboard? Some ideas to get you started:

restaurant signs
menus
airport signs
symbols and signs on airplanes
signs for pedestrians: bus stops, etc.
billboards advertising products
symbols for holidays: eggs, holly, flag
religious signs and symbols

On one entire wall in your classroom, make a giant collage of all the signs and symbols you can make or collect.

(178)

Each week let a trio of students take a Polaroid and photograph all the signs they can find in one afternoon. As these are brought back, put them on the wall. Each group will have to think a bit harder so as not to duplicate any already done. Students will be surprised at how many signs they have to read and understand every day. Possible places could include post office, hospital, beach, park, church, bus station, courthouse, etc.